The Sensible Guide to a Career in Project Management

in 2016

Dr. Te Wu

(PfMP®, PgMP®, PMP®, PMI-RMP®)

iExperi Press ▪ New York

The Sensible Guide to a Career in Project Management in 2016

Author: Te Wu
Editors: Bob Grieser, Brian Williamson
Publisher: iExperi Press

Published in the United States
ISBN-13: 978-1-941913-04-8
ISBN-10: 1-941913-04-0

Version 1.1
Printed by CreateSpace, a DBA of On-Demand Publishing LLC

DEDICATION

This book is dedicated to the students and professionals with whom I have had the honor and pleasure of working with as a teacher, mentor, team member, supervisor, or project leader. It is through working with you that I was inspired to write this book.

About the Author

Prof. Dr. Te Wu is the founder and CEO of PMO Advisory LLC, a management consulting firm specializing in strategic business execution and a PMI Global Registered Education Provider providing training in portfolio, program, project, agile, risk, and service management and project management office (PMO). Te has more than 20 years of experience in management consulting, having worked with industry leaders such as KPMG, Accenture, Oracle, Kraft, Standard and Poor's, Chase Bank, Corning Incorporated, and LexisNexis. He is an expert at implementing transformative change, enterprise resource planning (ERP), master data management (MDM), data analysis, and process optimization and simulation. For the past 14 years, Te has also held professorships at multiple universities in New Jersey and New York teaching international business, general management, organizational change, and project management. These include Stevens Institute of Technology, Touro Graduate School of Business, and Montclair State University. Te is one of an estimated 100 professionals worldwide certified in Portfolio (PfMP), Program (PgMP), Project (PMP), Risk (PMI-RMP) Management, and ITIL Foundation. In his spare time, he is working on a range of publications and research. Te also serves as a board member and in various advisory capacities for multiple educational institutions.

Table of Contents

List of Tables

List of Figures

Introduction

Project management is an exciting and growing field. The evidence of this exhilaration is all around us. Just witness the sheer speed of product evolution, not only in the technology world of smartphones and computing, but also in everyday life such as greener energy, innovation in food products, and the fabric of clothing that we wear. For those that like numbers, think about this. When the author became a certified Project Management Professional in 2003, there were less than 8,000 PMPs. Today, in April 2016, there are now over 714,000 PMPs, a compound annual growth rate (CAGR) of 14.3% for about a decade.

This book is written for aspiring and practicing project professionals at all levels. For students and entry-level professionals, this book introduces some of the key opportunities and challenges in this dynamic field. The book also presents a career road, which can serve as a guide post for growth. For senior project professionals, this book includes a discussion on advanced project management skills and also the latest PMI certifications and continuing credential requirements (CCRs) for portfolio, program, and project management.

i. Updates in the 2016 Edition

The author's goal is to update this book annually with major changes in the project management profession. As more organizations confront the resource scarcity and the necessity to accomplish more, project management and hence the number of project managers will inevitably grow. Furthermore, project management is a dynamic and growing discipline I include the latest developments in new concepts, practices, tools, and techniques.

The major updates to the 2016 edition of the book include the following:

- Inclusion of AXELOS' project related certifications including PRINCE2, MSP, and MoP
- PMI's new Talent Triangle including leadership, strategic, and technical skills
- PMI's continuing certification requirements for the eight PMI certifications
- PMI certification holder, including estimated, for end of 2016
- List of PMI chapters around the world
- List of project management resources (in Appendix B) including PMI, AXELOS, and PMO Advisory

ii. About The Sensible Guide

Sensible Guide is the title of a series of books and booklets designed with busy and smart people in mind. It strives to provide *highly relevant and exceedingly useful* information in the *right* context by providing explanations to the following:

- How to "do" something

- How to "use" something, and/or

- How to "think" about something

Having the right context is often more important than the content itself. Consequently, the Sensible Guides may be a bit lengthy in an attempt to provide a thorough understanding of context.

The Sensible Guides are also "open projects" as I plan to make frequent updates. I created a LinkedIn Group to support career and project management related questions. Feel free to join the group at https://www.linkedin.com/groups/8132544.

To register this book, please go to http://www.pmoadvisory.com/about-us/product-registration/. You will have an opportunity to be added to our mailing list for future product support.

Also, if you like this book and believe others can benefit, please provide us a testimonial at http://www.pmoadvisory.com/training/testimonials/ to help our marketing effort.

iii. About PMO Advisory LLC

Background

PMO Advisory LLC was founded in November 2012 by Te Wu, who tasked himself with creating the most specialized project management training and consulting firm, not only driven by business objectives (e.g. revenue and profit), but also with a strong social mission. Te's expertise spans multiple professions – throughout his multifaceted career he has worn many hats, including that of a management consultant, portfolio-/program-/project-/risk- manager, entrepreneur, business executive, and college professor.

As a teacher, Te works closely with students and recent graduates who are struggling to start their careers or unable to find meaningful work in their chosen fields. It was working in this capacity that Te was able to identify what he sees as one of the gravest social problems of our generation: the tremendous loss of professional jobs in developed countries due to technology, outsourcing, and offshoring. In Te's opinion, lack of jobs and underemployment has severely eroded the first rung of many professional career ladders. With an eye toward tackling this problem, Te founded PMO Advisory.

The problem of underemployment extends beyond recent graduates. There are many other disadvantaged groups, such as professionals over a certain age, veterans, and women in technology, and decent people who have had run-ins with the law and are being denied a second chance. Many of us are disadvantaged in one way or another.

Social Mission

This core of PMO Advisory's social mission is to "achieve human potential through work, education, and training." We believe in the power of work, which comprises so much of our sense of self-worth and accomplishment. We endeavor to enhance people's knowledge and experience through building human capital, increasing skills and marketability, and improving the competitiveness of our customers.

At PMO Advisory, we tackle this problem on many fronts. For our consulting clients, we "teach them how to fish," believing firmly in the future returns of empowerment and self-sufficiency over simply getting the job done. For individuals, we are pioneering programs that provide much-needed skills such as our Intelicamp, which helps make our customers more attractive in the marketplace.

As an aspiring B-Corporation (www.bcorporation.com), we believe that businesses should benefit all stakeholders and not just shareholders, and we are committed to finding solutions through socio-economic partnership.

Complimentary Resources

To promote our mission, PMO Advisory offers a wide range of free resources to our registered customers and potential customers. Currently, there are six categories of resources including:

- Assessments (e.g. PfMP Readiness)
- Books (e.g. this book and study aids)
- Social Media such as Linkedin Groups
- Online Demos (PMP, CAPM, Six Sigma, SCRUM, ITIL)
- Practice Exams (PMP, PgMP, and PfMP)
- Webinars (PMO, PMP, PgMP, PfMP, PMI-ACP and PMI-RMP)

NEWEST: Quicksheet for Project Managers – Free with product registration at www.pmoadvisory.com/about-us/product-registration.

The firm is also planning to enhance its social media presence and create a newsletter to keep our customers updated on the latest developments in project management.

To view and request these free resources or to sign-up for the newsletter, please go to http://www.pmoadvisory.com/free-resources

iv. Who Should Read This Book

Are you:

- A student figuring out your career ambitions and interested in learning more about project management? If so, follow **Terrance Lee**.

- A recent graduate beginning a career in project management? If so, follow **Patricia Johnson**.

- An experienced project manager working on large projects and endeavoring to advance your skills? If so, follow **Steve Jackson**.

- A project executive struggling to align your company's business implementation with strategy? If so, follow **Isabella Garcia**.

This book is designed for individuals at all levels of project management, from those who are just interested in learning about project professionals to those who want to explore the full range of project management disciplines associated with PMI certifications. To accompany the discussion of the project management profession, I have created four characters who are each at different stages of their careers. These characters are based on real people with whom I have had the honor of teaching or working with. By following these four characters and their journeys as they explore and progress in the field, I hope to develop for the reader a fully fleshed-out picture of the opportunities and challenges of the project management profession.

Meet Terrance Lee - A College Senior

Terrance Lee, a senior majoring in Management with a minor in Information and Technology, is contemplating which career to pursue. As the first in his family to attend college, he knows there are great expectations stemming from his immediate and extended family, including a close-knit group of high school buddies, neighbors, and friends from the community. Always very active and involved growing up, Terrance was considered an informal leader among his friends. Plus, as the oldest of four children, he is looked up to by his younger siblings. As he enters his senior year, the pressure is mounting for Terrance to land a solid job.

Terrance was attracted to management because he always wanted to build businesses, lead teams, and manage people. But after failing to secure his first choice of an internship last summer, his confidence was shaken. It also does not help that of the many positions he applied for, he received only a handful of noncommittal responses. On top of that, most positions were not particularly exciting, consisting of mainly administrative and clerical work. He pursued some management jobs as well, but was consistently told that these positions require real job experience. More than once now, Terrance has questioned whether he chose the right major.

Recently, he learned from his friends that they were enjoying a new elective class on project management. He was able to get a spot in the class right before the add/drop window closed, and is looking forward to his first class later in the week.

Meet Patricia Johnson - A Recent Graduate

Patricia Johnson is a recent college graduate with dual degrees in Art History and Finance. She works at a relatively small but growing marketing firm. She started as an intern in her junior year of college and has now been a financial analyst for the past three years. Patricia's career moved quickly in the first 20 months at the firm as her responsibilities increased steadily. But recently, she finds herself doing the same repetitive work. Though she still finds it interesting, she is coming to realize that she does not want to analyze numbers all her life. Plus, she wants to explore other parts of her firm, find ways to fuel her career, and progress faster.

Over a recent dinner with her friends, she overheard a conversation about a growing field called project management. She performed some quick research when she got home and was impressed at the number of hits on job sites. Then, just last night as she was watching TV, she was surprised to see National Car Rental's latest ad mentioning project management (www.ispot.tv/ad/72dl/national-car-rental-project-manager). Project management seems to be everywhere, and she is now really interested in moving her career in that direction. What should she do? How can she start?

Meet Steve Jackson – A Certified Project Management Professional (PMP)

Steve Jackson is a project manager on an enterprise resource planning (ERP) system implementation at a large financial services company. He is smart, ambitious, and has dozens of years of professional business experience under his belt, including the last eight years as a project manager. His career progression was quick, as he moved swiftly through the ranks from assistant to analyst and now vice president. He completed his Project Management Professional (PMP)® certification last year, and he thought he was fully ready to take on the management of the ERP implementation.

However, only three months into this three-year project, he is already overwhelmed. The overall project is still healthy, and each of the discrete sub-projects is still making progress. But Steve is worried. How will he bring these individual sub-projects together? Also, to his surprise, there are many more project tasks than originally conceived, which will make integration even harder. For example, while this project started as an IT systems implementation, the project is mired in business process design for the entire organization. The system architecture seems to be shifting constantly, and the most recent call with the data security group ended with another potential sub-project on ensuring data confidentiality and securing personally identifiable information (PII). Overburdened, Steve called his friend and mentor for the past dozen years to talk over the issues.

Isabella Garcia, a Senior Vice President with a global professional service firm, advised Steve to conceptualize the ERP project as a program – a large initiative with many moving parts that must come together at the end to deliver business benefits. Steve took Isabella's counsel to heart and started to explore the field of program management.

Meet Isabella Garcia – A Senior Project Executive

Isabella Garcia started her career as a chemist in a global pharmaceutical company. But a few years into her career as a scientist, she found herself becoming increasingly frustrated with her job. Upon introspection and analyzing her personality and interests, she became increasingly aware of her desire to work with people on new challenges across the organization in marketing, sales, manufacturing, supply chain management, and elsewhere. Thus, with her company's support, she finished her MBA in record time.

One of her early post-MBA assignments was working on a team to scale the production of a new drug. She performed so well on that project that she became the primary contact for other projects in her area. Now, many years later and with a few promotions and company changes, she is a SVP of a global consulting firm. Like many in her generation, she heard about the Project Management Institute and their certifications such as Project Management Professional (PMP), but she was not particularly interested in them as she had long outgrown those certifications.

Looking back, she recognizes that she is one of those "accidental project managers" who stumbled on the project management profession by chance. Even though there were many challenging projects in her career, including one she had to terminate due to insurmountable implementation difficulties, she considers herself fortunate. Scarred but toughened by numerous battle wounds, she is now groomed for the next level in her organization – heading the strategic project office where she will lead the governing team that makes all the crucial project investment decisions. She wonders to herself: Am I ready to manage this $100 million USD portfolio for my firm? How will I make sure these projects align and stay aligned with strategy? What about resource management – how will I best coordinate the capability and capacity of my organization?

v. Organization of This Book

This book is presented in five chapters

1. Introduction
2. Career in Project Management
3. Project Management Institute
4. Project Management Career Ladder
5. War Stories

Chapter 1: Introduction to the Field of Project Management

The first chapter provides an introduction to project management, as well as program and portfolio management. It addresses these five questions:

A. What are projects, programs, and portfolios?
B. What is project, program, and portfolio management?
C. Why project management?
D. How are projects different than operations?
E. Is project management a science or an art?

Chapter 2: Choosing a Career in Project Management

This chapter presents the challenges and opportunities of managing projects and whether it is the right profession for you. This chapter focuses on these three questions:

A. What are the challenges of project management?
B. What are the rewards of being a project manager?
C. Is project management right for you?

Chapter 3: Project Management Institute

Project Management Institute (PMI) is the world's largest project management professional organization dedicated to the advancement of the project management profession. For practitioners, it is a vital organization, not only for network and learning, but also for career development. PMI currently offers eight certifications designed for project professionals of all levels. Questions addressed in this chapter are as follows:

    A. What are PMI's certifications?
- What are the qualifications for each certification?
- Which one should you pursue?

    B. What do you need to do to maintain certifications?
    C. Are there other project management standards and certifications?

Chapter 4: Project Management Career Ladder

This chapter presents a general project management career ladder at three broad levels across seven titles. In addition, the chapter outlines 25 essential skills organized into three skills groups. Finally, I have included my thoughts on the skills, qualifications, and career development and certification strategies. The four questions discussed in this chapter are as follows:

    A. What does the project management career ladder look like?
    B. What are the core skills required to be an effective project managers?
    C. How does these skills map to the career ladder?
    D. Are there the core skills and qualification guidelines?

Chapter 5: War Stories

Synthesizing the content and strategies from the first four chapters, this chapter takes a different approach – storytelling. By presenting four stories from four individuals who are at different level of the project management profession, I hope to highlight selective project management concerns.

vi. Abbreviations and Acronyms

Throughout this book, I use abbreviations and acronyms for three reasons:

- Some acronyms have become a part of the natural language or are commonly used by project professionals and PMI. Therefore, they are important to know.
- Some tables are dense and place a heavy premium on the spacing
- Some concepts and names are long and used frequently

Table 1: Abbreviation and Acronyms

Abbreviation or Acronym	Description
CCR	Continuing Certification Requirement
CCRS	Continuing Certification Requirement System
ITTO	Input, tools and techniques, outputs (of portfolio processes)
MoP	Management of Portfolios
MSP	Managing Successful Programs
OPM3	Organizational Project Management
PfMP	Portfolio Management Professional
PgMP	Program Management Professional
PMBOK	Project Management Body of Knowledge
PMI	Project Management Institute
PMI-ACP	PMI Agile Certified Practitioner

Abbreviation or Acronym	Description
CCR	Continuing Certification Requirement
CCRS	Continuing Certification Requirement System
PMI-PBA	PMI Professional in Business Analysis
PMI-RMP	PMI Risk Management
PMI-SP	PMI Scheduling Professional
PMIS	Project-, program-, and portfolio management information system
PMP	Project Management Professional
PRINCE2	Projects IN Controlled Environments
R.E.P.	PMI's Registered Education Provider, a prestigious group of pre-approved training providers

vii. Common Project Management Terms

Like all professions, project management has developed a whole lexicon of its own jargon. Below are the words most commonly used to refer to the units of work required on projects. The approximate scale shows the *relative size* and *duration* of this work.

Table 2: Specific Project Terminology and Approximate Scale

Term	Description	Approx. Scale
Task or Activity	A piece of work that needs to be done. Project management favors the term "task" for projects and "activities" for operational work. But the distinction tends to be esoteric for non-project managers. For example, a task can be creating and reviewing a specific project plan and an operational activity can be updating a training manual as a part of ongoing management.	Hourly

Term	Description	Approx. Scale
Task Group, Work Group, Work Stream	A collection of tasks that is related and logically grouped together for ease of communication and management. For example, a task group can be creating a project schedule, and one of the tasks is reviewing a specific scheduling document.	Days / Weeks
Project	A one-time and often unique set of work designed to create changes. A project can be composed of many tasks and task groups coming together to create something meaningful. For example, the project of writing this book takes months, and it includes task groups like developing a project schedule which contains tasks such as reviewing a specific document.	Weeks / Months / Years

Term	Description	Approx. Scale
Program	A program is a logical collection of projects and occasionally operational activities that come together for management and the maximization of benefits. A program is often abstract and can contain multiple projects, sub-programs, and operational activities. For example, this book is a part of the larger program that my firm, PMO Advisory, is undertaking to create the most effective training programs.	Monthly, Annually, Multiple Years
Portfolio	A portfolio is a larger container that includes collections of programs, projects and operational activities. Portfolios should be aligned with business strategies to maximize the business value while minimizing negative risks. For example, this book is a part of the training program that, in time, will be a part of my firm's social mission portfolio. This portfolio of products strives to maximize the human experience through creating and delivering free, near-free, and/or highly effective products and services.	Multiple Years, Decades, some time for the duration of the organization unit

Term	Description	Approx. Scale
Project Management Office	A project management office, commonly known as a PMO, refers to an organizational unit responsible for a variety of centralized project management activities such as reporting, coordination, training, methodology, resource allocation, and project execution. Note: PMO can also refer to program- and portfolio management office. The term is usually not standardized in today's business environment. Thus, the specific activities and capabilities vary. PMO Advisory is a thought leader in this field, and we identified over 30 common PMO capabilities.	Ongoing

Chapter 1: Introduction to the Field of Project Management

.

"Most organizations are not facing shortages of ideas, even good ideas, they are starving for positive outcomes.

Project management is *the* discipline that achieves results!"

Te Wu

To understand why "projects" are becoming more and more important to the world and to get a sense of the pulse of project management, most people need not look further than their pockets or handbags. How many electronic devices do you normally carry? How often do you upgrade them? How frequently does the manufacturer release a new model? Every new model represents a project or a series of projects that comes together to comprise the device you are carrying. How do hundreds of components unite to form the latest smartphone, tablet, or a digital camera? The short answer is that each physical or software component represents a "project," and the management of these projects is called "project management." To use another analogy, have you ever planned a wedding or a big trip, worked with a team to build something, facilitated problem solving to overcome a big problem, or led a major client engagement? Chances are, you are already a project manager.

This chapter addresses these five questions:

- A. What are projects, programs, and portfolios?
- B. What is project, program, and portfolio management?
- C. Why project management?
- D. How are projects different than operations?
- E. Is project management a science or an art?

A. What are Projects, Programs, and Portfolios?

Projects are one-time and often unique sets of work designed to effect change or create something new. They are "one-time" because projects have start and end dates; they are "unique" because projects tend to create something different. Even if projects are repeated, such as annual fundraising campaigns, the factors surrounding the project – people, sponsors, locations, processes, goals and objectives - can vary from year to year.

Examples of projects occur everywhere, such as:

- New products - e.g. creating apps for Apple Watch
- Enhanced products - e.g. improving the battery in GM's Volt or improving a college curriculum
- Software – e.g. developing new applications
- Public Works – e.g. extending highways, completing construction
- Business Strategy –e.g. improving support ticket timely completion by 50%, reducing breakage in the food plant by 10%
- Students – e.g. pursuing a college or graduate degree, researching a thesis
- Personal – e.g. planning a major event, such as a wedding

If you want to sound like a project professional, then there are two other terms that you should know and use: program and portfolio. Programs are logical groupings of projects and even operational activities that collectively achieve a set of business benefits. For example, I previously helped a financial services company build a new servicing operation. The establishment of this new department consisted of multiple projects, such as system implementation, process design, hiring and training, and working with government regulators. This is considered a program because these projects are coordinated and integrated to achieve the ultimate business objective – creating a new department. By grouping similar projects and operational activities together, the program goal is to ensure alignment, create synergy, and maximize the efficiency and effectiveness of program implementation. Examples of programs include:

- New products – e.g. the successful launch of Apple Watch that includes the physical watch, 1000+ apps, and the entire marketing and sales campaign
- Business strategy – e.g. improving customer satisfaction from a net promoter score of 3 to 8 by the end of the year, which includes a project to improve support ticket timely completion

Project portfolios are even larger collections of programs, projects, and operational activities that achieve some common purpose while minimizing negativities. The concept is similar to financial portfolios, which many people have for their retirement. They share similar objectives such as maximizing gains at acceptable risks. The main difference between project portfolios and financial portfolios is primarily in the implementation. Most financial portfolio managers rely on others for the actual execution plus most financial portfolio managers concentrate on the financial piece only. In organizations, the project portfolio managers are also hands-on executives responsible for implementation. In addition to portfolio finances and budgets, project portfolio managers are responsible for governance, communication, monitoring implementation progress, and working with project and program managers. In this book, unless otherwise specified, "portfolio" always refers to project portfolios, not financial portfolios.

Examples of portfolios include:

- Wearable technology – e.g. managing all products and the associated value-added components such as apps; for Apple, this would include Apple Watch, Beats products, Nike partnership, apps, and other wearable products
- Business strategy – e.g. improving company profitability by focusing on customer acquisition and retention; in addition to a program for improving customer satisfaction, the portfolio includes additional programs and projects to attract new customers, enhance in-store experiences, improve product and service delivery, and create new reward programs

B. What is Project-, Program-, and Portfolio Management?

Project, program, and portfolio management is the application of knowledge, skills, tools, and techniques to implement projects, programs, and portfolios. Collectively, the three work hand-in-hand so that portfolios are *doing the right things* and programs and projects are *doing them in the right way*. Technically, project, program, and portfolio management are three distinct disciplines within the field of project management. As a matter of fact, the Project Management Institute offers three separate certifications for them.

However, in practice, much of the actual implementation tasks are related and intertwined.

Imagine an organization with hundreds of projects to complete. Which one should the firm undertake? Portfolio management is the discipline of collecting, categorizing, analyzing, prioritizing, approving (or rejecting), and monitoring portfolio components during implementation. To execute these portfolio components, portfolio managers create programs and projects. Program managers are typically more senior and seasoned professionals who have a greater scope of responsibility for achieving business benefits. Project managers are responsible for delivering project results.

It is important to recognize that some projects can be larger and more complex than programs, just as some projects can be bigger than portfolios. The convention commonly adopted is that a portfolio is the largest container, focusing on business or organization value; a program is the second-largest container, smaller than a portfolio but larger than a project, that concentrates on achieving specific benefits; a project is the smallest container narrowly focused on specific deliverables. That being said, understand that projects, programs, and portfolios are artificial constructs that project professionals create for the ease of communication and management.

To simplify the language in this book, henceforth the terms "project" and "project management" are used in a general way to represent all three specific disciplines of project, program, and portfolio management. Only when necessary, such as in Chapter 2 on PMI Certifications or in Chapter 4 on Career

Ladder, will the distinctions between project, program, and portfolio become relevant.

C. Why Project Management?

Why is project management gaining prominence? In my view, there are four primary reasons: 1) change; 2) competition; 3) a growing demand for improved products and services; 4) the relative effectiveness of project management at tackling complex initiatives.

This book is focused on the change brought about as a direct result of the competition spurred by globalization, the shift toward a more technology-oriented society, and other economic demands. Imagine the world of the mid-1940s. Most of the industrial world outside of North America was largely destroyed by the two World Wars. Largely unscathed by war, U.S. firms went on to dominant the world's consumer spending for the next two decades. But by the 1960s, the industrial strength of Europe and Japan was being rapidly revived. From the production of cars to televisions, the pace of competition increased steadily. In the 1970s and 1980s, the introduction of computers and digitization tracked an all-around rise in productivity levels, further fueling competition between businesses and countries. At the same time, a number of international bodies, such as the United Nations, the International Monetary Fund, and most importantly, the World Trade Organization, began to stabilize a new world order and encourage global trade. For these reasons, by the end of the 1980s, the world found itself in an age of booming competition.

We can witness this ever-increasing pace of change and competition all around us. According to Rita McGrath in "The Pace of Technology Adoption is Speeding Up," it took about five decades for the telephone to reach 50% of American households; the cell phone took only five years. In its earliest days, the automobile's design cycle was about 60 months; now, it's 24 to 36 months.[1] Businesses place a high premium on meeting the increasing consumer demand for the latest, new-and-improved products. Companies like Apple are expected to make significant enhancements to electronic gadgets like PCs, smartphones, and tablets and to churn these new models out with regularity. Samsung has upped the ante by releasing updated products even more quickly than Apple.

To cope with this increasing pace and cutthroat competition, organizations have searched for ways to improve its management. As a discipline, project management has its roots in the military. From the logistical planning of D-Day, which moved more than 150,000 personnel and millions of pieces of equipment across the English Channel, to managing the race to the moon, project management has made it possible for organizations to achieve major undertakings in ways that traditional operations cannot. Following the success of early project management, non-military projects in government sectors, corporations, and private companies began to use project management tools and processes to increase their effectiveness at implementing. As project management became more widely used, collective knowledge of tools and techniques led to its growth as a discipline.

D. How are Projects Different than Operations?

Projects and operational activities differ in two important ways. First off, projects are one-time sets of work with start and end dates, while operational activities comprise work that is routine and ongoing. Secondly, projects are unique, either in the deliverables, the means of implementation, or both. For operational activities, the deliverables and the means of implementation remain the same.

Let's look at an example. If an organization is always raising funds through their call center, then the call center work is operational. But if that same organization is implementing a new tool for better call management, this work would be considered a project. Still confused? Here's another way of deciphering the distinction between projects and operational activities. Think of an organization. What does it do? More specifically, what products does it sell or what services does it provide? If you are like me, and love cookies, one company that comes to mind is Mondelez (formerly Nabisco), which makes and sells cookies. Making and selling cookies enables Mondelez to make enough money to keep the bakery lights on. For a university like Montclair State University, keeping the lights on involves educating students; for Citibank, it is providing financial services to consumers and commercial organizations. Companies like Apple sell wonderful electronic gadgets like iPhones and services like iTunes. "Keeping the lights on" is generally accomplished by operational activities, which are highly repetitive, often routine, and performed by employees on an ongoing basis. But do these organizations sell the same products and services without ever changing them? The answer is an easy, "no." Imagine what Apple would look like if it were still selling the first generation iPhone while Samsung is putting its sixth generation smartphone on the market. To cope with changes both internal and external, Mondelez introduces new cookies, Montclair State creates new academic programs, Citibank develops new financial services products, and Apple constantly creates new and enhanced products like Apple Watch. The mechanism through which these changes are made is the project.

Once these projects have been completed, operational activities take over. For Mondelez, such activities include the baking, packing, distribution, and selling of cookies. For Citibank, it is servicing customers on the new financial products. Apple has its Genius Bar for answering questions and helping users. Operational activities are essential to creating new revenue for and returning profits to organizations; in turn, organizations funnel their profits into researching and developing new products and implementing them through projects. In this way, projects and operations form a complete virtual loop.

E. Is Project Management a Science or an Art?

Is project management a science or an art? The answer, unsurprisingly, is both. As a science, project management is the systematic application of knowledge, skills, tools, and techniques to efficiently and effectively manage the execution of a project. There are many tools and techniques, whose effectiveness has been proven through research and experimentation, that are available to project managers, such as Program Evaluation and Review Techniques (PERT), Earned Value Analysis (EVA), Gantt Charts, Critical Path Analysis, Critical Chain Project Management (CCPM), and Monte Carlo simulations. New research is continuously yielding new knowledge and tools to advance the field.

Traditionally, project management literature identifies three constraints called the Triple Constraint or Iron Triangle: schedule, cost, and scope. Schedule refers to the time required for a project to be implemented. Cost refers to a project's budget, including necessary talent and resources. Scope refers to a project's desired outcome or deliverables. As these three constraints tighten, a project's degree of difficulty increases and its probability of success decreases. The most challenging projects are when all three constraints are frozen; this makes success rather unlikely. Challenging projects often have two of the three constraints frozen. To make matters more complicated, real world projects often encompass additional constraints, such as quality of the project deliverables, organizational culture, especially in diverse and global environments, politics and power play, and even project management processes. The science of project management requires the careful management of these factors so that a project can be most effectively implemented.

But project management is also an art because projects are by nature complex, unstructured, subjective, and fraught with uncertainties. Politics, power, and special interests are often at play when it comes to projects. To effectively manage these complex projects, project management requires not just the scientific method; it requires professional judgment to make difficult choices, tenacity to make rapid decisions, perseverance to make it through challenging moments, and gumption to make unpopular choices. It is this gut-level intuition that elevates project management from a science to an art. Experienced project managers are not made in classrooms or by virtue of professional accreditations and certificates; they are made on the battleground and through the proverbial sweat and blood they shed over the course of a project. In my view, every great project manager must have failed at one point or another; success comes from risk-taking and the lessons learned through failure.

Another reason why project management resembles an art has to do with what I call the "principle of proportionality." Project management is popular precisely because of how effectively it manages complex endeavors. But what happens if the project management efforts become more labor-intensive than the problems it is seeking to fix? It is often easy for project managers without battle-tested experience and with a big budget to suggest rigorous project management structure, processes, tools, and techniques, losing sight of the ultimate goal. The art of project management lies in the finesse needed to apply just the right level of resources and processes to achieve an intended objective.

A final reason why project management is partially an art involves the "theory of good enough." Projects are fraught with conflicting demands and trade-offs required at every turn. It is easy for sponsors or customers to demand the "best" products or "perfect" solutions, but are they willing to pay the costs? When it comes to most products and services, more time spent on quality assurance will likely result in not only higher quality, but higher costs. Is the extra time and resources spent on achieving higher quality worth the extra effort on the part of the producer and the extra cost passed on to the consumer? Project deliverables must be "fit for use", but this concept is often subjective. For example, is two seconds a fast enough response time for an Internet application compared to a competitor's three seconds? Are the aesthetics of the latest gadget cool enough when compared with a competitor's product? When gauging such intangibles, it takes more intuitive artistry than methodical science to deem what is "good enough."

"When planning for a year, plant corn. When planning for a decade, plant trees. When planning for life, train and educate your mind, body, and spirit."

Adapted from a Chinese Proverb

Project management is not for everyone. As has already been discussed, projects can be unpredictable, complex, and stressful. Most project managers experience failure at some point in their careers. Yet the rewards of project management, both professional and personal, are undeniable. In this chapter, I will address three key career-related questions that will help you determine whether project management is right for you.

    A. What are the challenges of project management?
    B. What are the rewards of being a project manager?
    C. Is project management right for you?

A. What are the Challenges of Project Management?

To envision the challenges of project management, think of a pressure cooker. Pressure cookers are designed to cook food faster than almost any other cooking method. Raising the temperature of the cooker causes the pressure to increase within. The increased pressure, in turn, causes the water to become superheated steam, which cooks food more effectively and thus more quickly. A temperature of $100^{o}C$ in a pressure cooker is equivalent to $200^{o}C$ in a convection oven.

Now, let's apply this pressure cooker scenario to a project. An organization going about their projects as routine work is like cooking on an open stove. Work happens and progress is made, albeit slowly. Since there is little control of scope, the work is often open-ended as there is little control of the project outcomes. Time is not a key consideration, and resources are applied as needed. Organizations progress at their natural pace, which is often dictated by culture, resources, and other competing demands. Employees focus on their operational activities as their primary responsibilities and spare the little time they have on special initiatives like projects. If that organization is fine with the pace of progress, then there is nothing wrong with this "open stove" approach.

But what happens when *urgency* enters the picture? Let's say a competitor just released a new product that is significantly superior to the organization's own. Or, let's say a government deadline for compliance is looming. What's an "open stove" organization to do? The answer is, take out the pressure cooker!

In this scenario, time becomes an important variable. Schedules must be shortened. Scope needs to be limited. The cooking process is no longer an open pot in which everyone can toss in their ingredients willy-nilly. Even the largest pressure cooker can only hold so many ingredients! Budget is now a concern too, and funding becomes necessary to afford the ingredients and the proper size and quality of the pressure cooker. Here we've arrived at the classic triplet of constraints: cost, schedule, and scope. But there is much more. The energy source must be increased to enable faster cooking. Energy, in this case, is equivalent to resources. Quality of cooking is much more difficult to control in a superheated environment, which is a systemic problem of a shortened schedule. The different ingredients, which were to be so elegantly arranged in an open pot on the stove, now intermingle at an accelerated rate producing unintended flavors. The chef, which was used to watching the news while cooking now has to diligently maintain a keen eye on the cooking process at all times. For the chef, our metaphorical project manager, overcooking even by a minute can have disastrous consequences. Worse, once the lid is on, it is difficult to add new ingredients. Through this pressure cooker analogy, you can see how the challenges of project management – schedule, cost, scope, resources, culture, and leadership – play out.

Keep in mind that the description offered here is designed to provide a general sense of the challenges of project management. Throughout this book, especially in Chapter 5, I will present additional project challenges.

B. What are the Rewards of Being a Project Manager?

In my experience, the project management profession is relatively high-risk and high-stress. There are certainly higher stakes professions such as medical doctors, emergency responders, or even investment bankers. These professions aside, project managers have to endure more stress than most other professions – they're constantly managing pressure cookers, after all.

The rewards, however, are undeniable. The old adage, "Fortune favors the brave" surely applies to project managers. Here I will give you six big reasons why a career in project management is rewarding:

    i.   Seldom boring
    ii.   Opportunities to celebrate
    iii.   Excellent compensation
    iv.   Marketable skills
    v.   Rapid job growth
    vi.   Support by the Project Management Institute

i. Seldom Boring

Projects, by nature, are unique. Project managers confront a wide array of challenges and become intimately familiar with Murphy's Law, which states that "anything that can go wrong, will go wrong." I would even extend this further with the project management corollary to Murphy's Law, and suggest that "even those things that don't usually go wrong can also go wrong." Consequently, most project managers are well-versed in the art of making order out of chaos. While these situations can be extremely challenging, they are rarely tedious. It's no surprise that, in all my years of working with project managers, I've heard few, if any, complaints of boredom.

ii. Plenty of Opportunities to Celebrate

On complex and large projects, project managers put out one fire after another. The flip side of these challenges is that there are many opportunities to celebrate wins, small and large alike. With experience and some good fortune, astute project managers learn how to exploit crises and turn them into opportunities. Even significant project failures, as long as they are not catastrophic and irreversible, can be fodder for learning, improvement, and growth. Project managers should also act as cheerleaders in charge and there is often plenty of progress to celebrate. For people who like to feel accomplished, project management will give you that satisfaction.

iii. Excellent Compensation

In PMI Salary Survey 2015[2], which surveyed over 26,000 project management professionals globally, it found that project professionals with PMP (or other PMI certifications) earn significantly more than project professionals without certification in all countries but two. Here is a summary of the findings:

- The highest gap is South Africa with PMPs earning $72,267 and non-PMPs earning $49,142, a difference of 47%.
- Poland shows the greatest % increase at 25%. PMPs earn $40,310 and non-PMPs earn $32,254.
- The United States shows a 22% increase with PMPs earning $111,000 and non-PMPs earning $91,000.
- The only two countries with a % increase at zero or negative are Japan and Sweden.

This finding is consistent with other surveys. For example, according to a 2013 survey by ESI International[3], the average starting salary for project managers is $54,593 and jumps significantly to $103,047 for senior project managers. By my estimation, the average starting salary for project managers in 2015 is $58,178[4]. This easily tops the salary chart for all business majors.

Table 3: Starting Salary for Business Majors at the Bachelor's Level[5]

Major	Average Starting Salary in 2015
Project Management (estimated)	$58,178
Management Information System	$55,843
Logistics /Supply Chain	$53,024
Finance	$52,788
Accounting	$51,475
Business Administration / Management	$51,196
Sales	$50,200
Marketing	$49,419

There are other studies that support this finding. According to *Forbes* in an article entitled "10 High-Paying Flexible Jobs,"[6] senior project managers in information technology top the list at $99,700 a year on average. Furthermore, and a big boon for work-life balance, 26% of these professionals claim that they are able to do their jobs from home. This compares very favorably to the 7% for all jobs and industries with at least a bachelor's degree that are able to work from home.

iv. Marketable Skills

Project management skills are in great demand. I agree with the Project Management Institute (PMI) in their assertion that project management abilities are both specific management and life skills. In the current edition of PMI's *Project Management Body of Knowledge*, there are ten knowledge areas: scope, schedule, cost, quality, procurement, risk, communication, stakeholder, human resources, and integration management. This does not include additional commonly accepted skill domains, such as issue, change, conflict, team, cross-functional, and cross-cultural management. Project managers must also balance strategic perspectives with hands-on management deliverables. Senior project managers must operate at multiple levels, from strategy to execution. Those who are able to synthesize skills successfully are inevitably some of the most successful professionals. Is it any wonder, then, that solid project managers are highly marketable and in great demand?

v. Rapid Job Growth

The growth of the business management profession can be seen in the number of hits on job sites, as organizations seek out project managers to stay ahead of competition. There are many metrics with which to measure job growth, but perhaps the most telling is the increase in PMI membership. With 215,367 members in late November 2006, the membership experienced a compound annual growth rate (CAGR) of nearly

9% to 477,992 members by April of 2016. The growth in holders of its most popular credential, Project Management Professional (PMP), is even more astonishing, with an increase from 206,774 to 714,431, or a CAGR of 14.3%.

Here, the astute reader might ask why there are more PMP credential holders (714,431) than there are PMI members (477,992). I spoke with a PMI employee at the North America Global Congress, and she confirmed my suspicion. Many members, especially from non-English speaking countries, do not consistently maintain their PMI membership. They only join when it is time to renew their certifications, which is typically good for three years. Thus, they let their membership lapse for two years before repeating this cycle. The reason that members from non-English speaking countries cancel more frequently is due to a lack of content.

This book provides a much greater analysis of PMI certifications in the next chapter. To see the average annual increase of PMI certifications, go to Table 5: Average Annual Increase of PMI Certifications. To review the year-by-year increase in PMI membership, PMBOK publication, and PMI certifications, go to Figure 3: PMI Annual Membership & Certification Growth Rate (2006 - 2016 Estimated).

vi. Support by Project Management Institute

Aside from a number of popular professions such as physicians, accountants, and lawyers, very few professions have the support of a major professional organization. Since its establishment in 1969, the Project Management Institute has arguably done more to establish project management as an important business profession than any other project professional organization. In addition to establishing standards such as the Project Management Body of Knowledge, Standard for Program Management, and Standard for Portfolio Management, PMI has grown an entire ecosystem for project managers, ranging from research to continuing education.

The major certifications, starting with Certified Associate in Project Management (CAPM) to Portfolio Management Professional (PfMP) track a career path that can easily span 20 years or more. As a chapter leader in New York City, I am familiar with initiatives to make CAPM available to high school students. When PMI established the Portfolio Management Professional (PfMP), they closed the gap between strategy and execution. By using portfolio management to ensure that organizations select the right projects, and by using program and project management to ensure the proper execution of these projects, PMI has created a virtuous cycle linking ideas to reality.

Despite the many challenges associated with project management as discussed throughout this book, very few professions are supported by as lively and dynamic an organization as PMI, which boasts active members all around the world. I've personally benefited from the support offered by PMI, having attended the New Orleans Leadership Institute Meeting (LIM) in 2013 and the North America Congress in

Phoenix, Arizona in October 2014. The opportunities to network, learn, and collaborate are truly amazing.

C. Is Project Management Right for You?

Project management is surely not for everyone. Project managers require a healthy capacity for learning, as projects are unique and often demand specialized knowledge and skills. They must also have a propensity for challenges and risk-taking, which can be stressful. Perhaps the most difficult palate is the inevitability of failure for project managers. Nobody possesses the superhuman powers needed to salvage every situation. As I often jokingly tell my students, "to make a cup of freshly squeezed orange juice, you need oranges - and preferably juicy ones, too." Project managers will likely encounter some impossible situations over the course of their careers in which their managers or customers demand the impossible. Sound challenging? Take this quick aptitude test to ascertain whether or not you are suited to be a project manager.

Instructions:

The table below contains a list of ten common project characteristics. Honestly answer how comfortable you feel about each item using a simple scale of 1 to 3, where: 1 = Uncomfortable, 2 = Neutral, 3 = Comfortable

#	Question	Points
1	Coping with unstructured work	
2	Taking risks	
3	Handling politics	
4	Putting out fires	
5	Making unpopular choices	
6	Managing change and surprises	
7	Relying on other's expertise	
8	Solving problem, often without precedent	
9	Tackling conflicts	
10	Leading teams and taking charge	
Score (add the points):		

What is your score? If you score:

Score	Description
12 or below	Project management is not likely to be your favorite profession. Though you may be able to do the job, you will not likely enjoy its many challenges.
13-18	You should consider taking a closer look at project management. While there are some attributes to the profession that you will not prefer, you may be able to minimize these negatives in some situations.
19-23	You should definitely consider taking a closer look at project management. Clearly, there are

Score	Description
	some attributes of the job that you are comfortable with. See how you might be able to maximize the characteristics you prefer and minimize those that you are uncomfortable with.
24-27	Project management is likely to be an excellent career choice for you! Continue to explore the profession and where your greatest strengths might lie.
28-30	Project management appears to be a profession tailor-made for you! I highly encourage you to fully explore this profession. In all likelihood, you will be a great project manager.

3. Project Management Institute (PMI)

"It's not enough that we do our best; sometimes we have to do what's required."

Winston Churchill

The Project Management Institute (PMI®) is the world's largest not-for-profit project management professional organization dedicated to supporting and advancing the project management profession, which includes project, program, and portfolio management. Founded in 1969, PMI is serving the field of project management by creating and formalizing standards, developing new knowledge through research and collaboration, spreading the benefits of project management through its marketing and outreach efforts, educating its members through training programs and conferences, and building the profession through grassroots activities.

According to the April 2016 issue of *PMI Today*, one of PMI's publications, there are 477,992 members around the world and across 278 chapters, organized in the four regions shown in Figure 1 below. Its most popular certification is the Project Management Professional (PMP®), with over 714,431 credential holders. To date, the Project Management Body of Knowledge (PMBOK®) has nearly 5.2 million copies in circulation. For a complete listing of PMI chapters and potential chapters as of December 2015, refer to Appendix A.

For project management practitioners in the United States and Canada, it is relatively easy to find PMI chapters. In the United States alone, there are roughly 148 chapters. Canada has 18 Chapters.

Figure 1: PMI Chapters and Potential Chapters Around the World

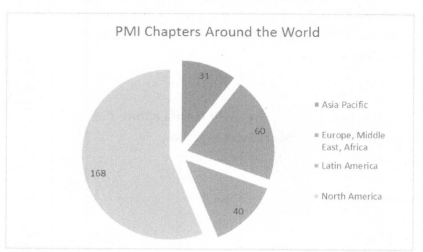

This chapter will address the following questions about the Project Management Institute:

A. What are PMI's certifications?
- What are the qualifications for each certification?
- Which one should you pursue?
B. What do you need to do to maintain certifications?
C. Are there other project management standards and certifications?

A. What are PMI's certifications?

While PMI currently offers nine certifications, I will only discuss only eight in this book. The ninth certification, Organizational Project Management Maturity Model or OPM3, is somewhat controversial with a relatively small number of certified members. (Though PMI does not publish the number of credential holders, the informal estimate is less than 70 worldwide.)

The table below shows the eight certifications and the respective number of credential holders.

Table 4: Project Management Institute's Eight Certifications and Number of Credential Holders (March 2015)[7]

#	Certification Name	Number of Active Credential Holders
1	CAPM or Certified Associate in Project Management®	30,830
2	PgMP or Program Management Professional®	1,528
3	PfMP or Portfolio Management Professional®	301
4	PMP or Project Management Professional®	714,431
5	PMI-ACP or Agile Certified Professional®	10,898
6	PMI-RMP or Risk Management Professional®	3,523
7	PMI-SP or Scheduling Professional®	1,478
8	PMI-PBA or Professionals in Business Analysis®	634

Figure 2: Total PMI Credential Holders (April 2016)

By becoming a certified professional, you join the ranks of a growing network of project professionals. The rapid increase of certifications issued is evident in the table below, which tracks the average annual increase in certification holders from 2014 to 2016 (projection based on actual data as of April 2016).

Table 5: Average Annual Increase of PMI Certifications

Certification Name	Start Date	# of Credential Holders on Start Date	# of Credential Holders in April 2016	Average Annual Increase
CAPM	Nov-06	1,438	30,830	25%
PMP	Nov-06	206,774	714,431	13%
PgMP	Dec-10	492	1,528	20%
PfMP	Dec-13	162	301	40%
PMI-ACP	Dec-12	1,611	10,898	40%
PMI-RMP	Dec-10	516	3,523	27%
PMI-SP	Dec-10	377	1,478	21%
PMI-PBA	Dec-14	182	634	71%

The Start Date as listed in the table above marks the earliest date on which I was able to find reliable data. With the exception for CAPM and PMP, for which I could not obtain earlier information, the Start Date for all other certification is the last month of the first year in which the certification was offered.

Figure 3: PMI Annual Membership & Certification Growth Rate (2006 - 2016 Estimated)

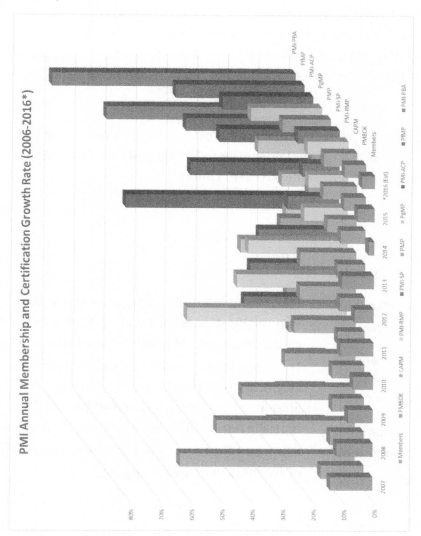

As you can see from Figure 3, PMI is maturing and therefore its growth rate is beginning to decelerate. But PMI is constantly seeking out new ways to branch out. In 2013, PMI introduced the Portfolio Management Professional; in 2014, it founded the Professional in Business Analysis (PMI-PBA) certification. In 2015, as this book is being written, PMI is reworking the Continuing Certification Requirement (CCR) program to ensure continual relevance and value to the profession.

In the following section, I will provide brief descriptions of the professional certifications. The following table outlines the major attributes of each certification.

Table 6: Summary Table for PMI Certification

A. Qualifications	
Secondary Degree	The minimum educational requirement for all PMI certification is a secondary degree or the global equivalent of a high school diploma.
Advanced Degree	The amount of experience required for some certifications differs depending on the amount of education. Advanced degrees typically require 40% less work experience.
Additional Requirement	Some certifications have additional education or business experience requirements.

B. Certification Fees (First Time, Re-Exam, and CCR)	
Exam Fees for CBT (Member/Non-Member)	PMI exams are typically offered as computer-based testing (CBT), but paper-based tests are administered in special circumstances. This book will primarily cover CBT. For more information on the paper-based testing, refer to the certification handbook, as listed at the bottom of the table. PMI fees are significantly lower for members than non-members. As discussed briefly in Chapter 2, this may explain why there are more PMPs than PMI members. For you, it is usually more cost effective to be a PMI member when you are applying for certifications and renewals.
Re-Exam Fees for CBT (Member/Non-Member)	
CCR Renewal (Member/Non-Member)	
C. Certification Exam	
# of Questions (Scored / Pre-Test/ Total)	All PMI certification exams are based on a series of questions. Depending on the certification, the questions can be knowledge- and experience-based. Mathematical calculations are often required. In a CBT testing environment, the testing software provides a calculator.
Allocated Time for Exam in Hours	On each of the exams, about 11-20% of the questions are pre-test questions. These are future questions that PMI is including for testing and validation. These questions are not scored. However, since you do not know which question is a scored versus the pre-test

	question, you have to treat them with equal attention.
Approx. Time per Question in Seconds	Based on the number of questions and the allocated time, I calculated the approximate time per question. This is used to demonstrate the relatively high pressure exam environment.
Language Aid	On popular exams, such as PMP, PMI provides additional language aids.

D. Continual Certification Requirement

Certification Period in Years	Once you have satisfactorily completed the exam and the credential process, the certifications are good for three years, except CAPM which is good for five years.
Total # of PDUs	With the exception of CAPM, which is not renewable, maintaining certifications require continual development. PMI's Continuing Certification Requirements (CCR) program supports the ongoing learning and professional development by earning Professional Development Units (PDUs).
# of PDUs in Education	
# of PDUs in Giving Back	PDUs are awarded in two broad categories: Education and Giving Back to the Profession.

PDU Transfer to Next Period	Education is based on the new PMI Talent Triangle™ with three categories of skill sets: technical project management, leadership, and strategic and business management.
Additional Remarks	Giving back to the profession are activities contributing to the vitality of the profession. This includes volunteering, creating new knowledge and content, giving a presentation, sharing knowledge and working as a professional.
	If you earn more PDUs than is required for a period, you can transfer a portion to the next period. Only PDUs earned within the 12 months of the certification cycle can be applied to the next cycle.
When Should You Pursue this Certification?	Since this table provides only a summary of the certification information, the URL for each of the certification handbooks is included here for your reference.
URL for Handbook	

- The PMI Talent Triangle focuses on professional development in three key areas:
- Technical Project Management – This domain concentrates on the specialized skills required for each certifications. For example, technical skills can include agile practices, data gathering, creating detailed project plans, analyzing risks, and developing performance metrics.

- Leadership – This domain focuses on competencies related to guiding, motivating, and leading people and organizations. Specific skills include coaching and mentoring, brainstorming, resolving conflicts, negotiation, and building teams.
- Strategic and Business Management – Projects do not exist in a vacuum, and PMI now dedicates special attention to making sure projects are intimately linked to the broader business environment. This domain emphasizes business oriented skills such as managing benefits, general business acumen and knowledge, competitive analysis, functional knowledge of various operational units, and strategic planning.

In general, for certifications such as PMP, a minimum of eight (8) PDUs are required in each of the three domain areas.

i. Certified Associate in Project Management (CAPM)

CAPM is an entry-level certification designed for project practitioners and high school, undergraduate, and graduate students who have little to no experience in project management but wish to learn more. The certification demonstrates an understanding of the core concepts, tools and techniques, and processes of project management.

Table 7: Certified Associate in Project Management (CAPM) Summary

A. Qualifications	
Secondary Degree	1,500 hrs of project experience
Advanced Degree	Not Required
Additional Requirement	23 hours of education
B. Certification Fees (First Time, Re-Exam, and CCR)	
Exam Fees for CBT (Member/Non-Member)	$225 or €185 / $300 or €250
Re-Exam Fees for CBT (Member/Non-Member)	$150 or €125 / $200 or €170
CCR Renewal (Member/Non-Member)	$225 or €185 / $300 or €250
C. Certification Exam	
# of Questions (Scored / Pre-Test/ Total)	135 / 15 / 150
Allocated Time for Exam in Hours	3
Approx. Time per Question in Seconds	72
Language Aid	13
D. Continual Certification Requirement	
Certification Period in Years	5
Total # of PDUs	Not applicable
# of PDUs in Education	Not applicable

# of PDUs in Giving Back	Not applicable
PDU Transfer to Next Period	Not applicable
Additional Remarks	Expires automatically in 5 years, unless you re-certify
When Should You Pursue this Certification?	Pursue this early in your career. The rewards are especially great at the entry-level
URL for Handbook	http://www.pmi.org/Certification/ ~/media/PDF/Certifications/pdc_c apmhandbook.ashx

Personally, I have been ambivalent for years about the desirability of the CAPM certification. On the one hand, CAPM is not widely recognized in the industry. Plus, many professionals may have many years of experience but spread among many disciplines other than project management. Having an "entry-level" project management certificate may inadvertently damage their professional credibility. On the positive side, for entry-level professionals and students, attaining CAPM can be a significant boost to your credentials. It demonstrates to your employer that you're serious about the profession and your career. Plus, the certification is gaining popularity.

ii. Project Management Professional (PMP)

PMP is the most popular project management certification in the world today. There are sixteen times more active PMP certificate holders than all the other PMI certifications combined. For most organizations, PMP is the gold standard and represents a strong understanding and application of project management.

When I first obtained my PMP in 2003, the market value was significantly higher than it is today. Then, to hold a PMP was seen as a competitive advantage. Today, sadly, I believe the popularity of the certification has diluted its professional value. Now, it is more commonly seen as a competitive parity, especially in the information technology industry where there is the highest concentration of PMPs.

Nonetheless, even if it is only competitive parity, the importance of attaining the PMP cannot be overstated. A PMI survey in 2015 shows an increase of $20,000 USD for professionals with PMP versus without it, in the United States. While this number may not be achieved in all situations, professionals with PMP clearly have some advantage over the non-certified professionals, assuming all other factors are equal.

Table 8: Project Management Professional (PMP) Summary

A. Qualifications	
Secondary Degree	Five years of project management experience + 7,500 hours leading and directing projects
Advanced Degree	Three years of project management experience + 4,500 hours leading and directing projects

Additional Requirement	35 hours of education
B. Certification Fees (First Time, Re-Exam, and CCR)	
Exam Fees for CBT (Member/Non-Member)	$405 or €340 / $555 or €465
Re-Exam Fees for CBT (Member/Non-Member)	$275 or €230 / $375 or €315
CCR Renewal (Member/Non-Member)	$60 / $150
C. Certification Exam	
# of Questions (Scored / Pre-Test/ Total)	175 / 25 / 200
Allocated Time for Exam in Hours	4
Approx. Time per Question in Seconds	72
Language Aid	13
D. Continual Certification Requirement	
Certification Period in Years	3
Total # of PDUs	60
# of PDUs in Education	Minimum 35 PDUs overall with a minimum of 8 PDUs from Technical, Leadership, and Strategic areas. The remaining 11 can be across any of the PMI Talent Triangle.

# of PDUs in Giving Back	Maximum 25
PDU Transfer to Next Period	Up to 20 PDUs earned in the final 12 months of the certification cycle.
Additional Remark	PMP and PgMP can generally share their PDUs
When Should You Pursue this Certification?	Pursue this when you are ready to independently lead projects, even if they are smaller initiatives
URL for Handbook	http://www.pmi.org/Certification /~/media/PDF/Certifications/pdc_ pmphandbook.ashx

As project management matures, the Project Management Profession (PMP) is not just desirable but a necessity. Look at the world from a hiring manager's perspective. It is often genuinely difficult to make hiring selections with competing candidates. Much of the candidate evaluation criteria is subjective, but whether a candidate has PMP is a concrete data point.

For up-and-coming project managers, PMP is even more important. In addition to providing an important (and, perhaps, the most important) credential, studying the project management body of knowledge helped me and many others organize and solidify the experiences, skills, tools, techniques, and artifacts of project management. Learning the materials also creates a common language that can make for better communication not only among project managers but among project teams.

iii. Program Management Professional (PgMP)

PMI introduced the Program Management Professional (PgMP) certification in 2007 to create a new gold standard for senior and experienced project and program professionals. The original certification was an expensive and tedious three step process. The third-step, called "multi-rater assessment," was especially onerous. For these and other reasons, PgMP did not grow as quickly as anticipated. Recently, PMI simplified the certification into a 2-step process, aligning it with all other PMI certifications.

In PMI's world, program management is viewed as a distinct profession from project management. Program management is not only ranked at a higher level, but its considerations are also different, including strategic alignment, benefits management, and governance. In the market, the line between programs and large projects are often blurred, but program management is viewed as a higher level of management than project management. Program components include projects, operational initiatives, and occasionally smaller programs that must collectively come together to deliver a set of business benefits. Therefore, for most project managers looking to gain increased responsibility and recognition, PgMP is a logical next step.

Table 9: Program Management Professional (PgMP) Summary

A. Qualifications	
Secondary Degree	Four years (6,000 hours) of project management experience + seven years (10,500 hours) of program management experience
Advanced Degree	Four years (6,000 hours) of project management experience + four years (6,000 hours) of program management experience
Additional Requirement	
B. Certification Fees (First Time, Re-Exam, and CCR)	
Exam Fees for CBT (Member/Non-Member)	$800 or €655 / $1,000 or €815
Re-Exam Fees for CBT (Member/Non-Member)	$600 or €490 / $800 or €655
CCR Renewal (Member/Non-Member)	$60 / $150
C. Certification Exam	
# of Questions (Scored / Pre-Test/ Total)	150 / 20 / 170
Allocated Time for Exam in Hours	4
Approx. Time per Question in Seconds	84.7
Language Aid	1

D. Continual Certification Requirement	
Certification Period in Years	3
Total # of PDUs	60
# of PDUs in Education	Minimum 35 PDUs overall with a minimum of 8 PDUs from Technical, Leadership, and Strategic areas. The remaining 11 can be across any of the PMI Talent Triangle.
# of PDUs in Giving Back	Maximum 25
PDU Transfer to Next Period	Up to 20 PDUs earned in the final 12 months of the certification cycle
Additional Remark	PMP and PgMP can generally share their PDUs
When Should You Pursue this Certification?	PgMP is ideal for a seasoned project manager who is confident in his/her ability to manage complex projects and programs
URL for Handbook	http://www.pmi.org/~/media/PDF/Certifications/pdc_pgmphandbook.ashx

As the market has becoming crowded with PMPs, the program management credential is now viewed as one of the certifications that provides a competitive advantage. For senior project professionals, the advantage of PgMP will likely last for many years to come.

iv. Portfolio Management Professional (PfMP)

I was excited when PfMP was first announced in the summer of 2013. As a practicing portfolio manager, I had been an advocate for the advancement of the profession. To me, one of the greatest organizational challenges is business execution. For firms to be successful, they must first invest in the right projects. The missing link between strategy and execution is the project portfolio manager. I joined the pilot group immediately and took the PfMP exam on January 4th, 2014. When the pilot result was announced, to my surprise and joy, I was one of the first ten people in the world to receive the certification. This initiated my firm's journey toward developing a suite of PfMP products, and my firm became the first company to introduce bootcamps for PfMP, PgMP, and PMP.

There was an additional surprise in the announcement of the PfMP pilot results. Of the first 121 people certified, almost 50%, or 59 people, of those who completed the certification did not have any other major PMI certifications. I explored the rationale why, and in my conversation with many portfolio managers, here are the top three reasons that I have unearthed:

1. Many senior project executives became project managers "by accident." They started working on projects before project management as a profession became popular. Along the way, they gained greater and greater responsibilities. When PMP became more

popular, these senior executives had grown beyond the need for the PMP. But portfolio management certification is a new advancement.

2. These senior project executives had been yearning for a certification that is more meaningful to their career. PfMP is precisely that.

3. The PfMP certification is viewed as the pinnacle of the project management profession. This creates a unique advantage that is likely to last for the remainder of one's career.

Table 10: Portfolio Management Professional (PfMP) Summary

A. Qualifications	
Secondary Degree	Seven years (10,500 hours) of portfolio management experience within the past 15 consecutive years
Advanced Degree	Four years (6,000 hours) of portfolio management experience within the past 15 consecutive years
Additional Requirement	Eight years (96 months) of professional business experience
B. Certification Fees (First Time, Re-Exam, and CCR)	
Exam Fees for CBT (Member/Non-Member)	$800 or €655 / $1,000 or €815

Re-Exam Fees for CBT (Member/Non-Member)	$600 or €490 / $800 or €655
CCR Renewal (Member/Non-Member)	$60 / $150
C. Certification Exam	
# of Questions (Scored / Pre-Test/ Total)	150 / 20 / 170
Allocated Time for Exam in Hours	4
Approx. Time per Question in Seconds	84.7
Language Aid	1
D. Continual Certification Requirement	
Certification Period in Years	3
Total # of PDUs	60
# of PDUs in Education	Minimum 35 PDUs overall with a minimum of 8 PDUs from Technical, Leadership, and Strategic areas. The remaining 11 can be across any of the PMI Talent Triangle.
# of PDUs in Giving Back	Maximum 25
PDU Transfer to Next Period	Up to 20 PDUs earned in the final 12 months of the certification cycle

Additional Remark	PfMP PDUs must be specialized in portfolio management
When Should You Pursue this Certification?	PfMP is for project executives who desire to have greater influence over an organization's project direction. But be ready to play with politics and power struggles!
URL for Handbook	http://www.pmi.org/Certificatio n/~/media/PDF/Certifications/pf mphandbook.ashx

As the senior-most certification currently in the Project Management Institute's family of project management certifications, PfMP is perfect for senior project executives who want to demonstrate their vast experience and superior qualifications. More importantly, for the general business world, portfolio management resolves the major discrepancy between strategy and execution. The table below contains some of the recent studies, including a March 2015 article in *Harvard Business Review*, about the failure and challenges of strategic business execution.

Table 11: Recent Studies on Business Execution

#	Finding	Reference
1	Half or more strategic initiatives fail	Miller, Hickson, and Wilson, 2008[viii]

#	Finding	Reference
2	90%, or 9 out of 10, strategic implementations fail	Speculand, 2009[ix]
3	61% of executives acknowledge that their firms often struggle to bridge the gap between strategy formulation and implementation. In 2012, just 56% of strategic initiatives were successful (in other words, 44% of strategic initiatives failed)	Economist Intelligence Unit, 2013[x]
4	70% of strategic plans and strategies are never successfully implemented	Corboy and O'Corrbui, 1999[xi]
5	70% of all change initiatives fail	Beer and Nohria, 2000[xii]
6	The real success rate of successfully implementing strategic plans is only 10% to 30%; this low rate is discouraging, especially since a growing number of companies in recent years have invested considerable resources in developing strategic planning skills	Raps, 2004[xiii]
7	A recent survey of 400 global CEOs found that executional excellence is the number one challenge facing business leaders across the globe	Sull, Homkes, and Sull, 2015[xiv]

If you are a senior project professional responsible for selecting, prioritizing, approving, and managing a portfolio of projects in your organization, PfMP is a vital certification that establishes your qualifications. The studies above are just a small sampling of recent research that consistently points to the failure of business execution. Portfolio managers alone cannot solve all of the problems of business execution, but by helping organizations to "do the right things," the value of portfolio management is abundantly clear.

v. PMI Professional in Business Analysis (PMI-PBA)

In 2014, the Project Management Institute ventured into another common role of projects: business analyst. According to statistics from the U.S. Department of Labor, the number of business analyst jobs in the United States will likely increase 19% by 2022[xv]. An informal examination of job roles and requirements in the New York City metro area shows that business analyst jobs are among the most popular in the region.

This certification runs parallel to the Project Management Professional (PMP). In the industry today, business analysts and project managers are two vital roles, especially for information technology projects. As business analysts gain experience, they often become project managers. But successful project managers often have strong skill sets in business analysis, as project managers must understand business challenges and navigate change.

Table 12: PMI Professional in Business Analysis (PMI-PBA) Summary

A. Qualifications	
Secondary Degree	7,500 hours or 5 years working as a practitioner within the last 8 years + 2,000 hours of project experience, which can include the 7,500 hours above
Advanced Degree	4,500 hours or 3 years working as a practitioner within the last 8 years + 2,000 hours of project experience, which can include the 4,500 hours above
Additional Requirement	35 hours of training in business analysis
B. Certification Fees (First Time, Re-Exam, and CCR)	
Exam Fees for CBT (Member/Non-Member)	$405 or €340 / $555 or €465
Re-Exam Fees for CBT (Member/Non-Member)	$275 or €230 / $375 or €315
CCR Renewal (Member/Non-Member)	$60 / $150
C. Certification Exam	

# of Questions (Scored / Pre-Test/ Total)	175 / 25 / 200
Allocated Time for Exam in Hours	4
Approx. Time per Question in Seconds	72
Language Aid	1
D. Continual Certification Requirement	
Certification Period in Years	3
Total # of PDUs	60
# of PDUs in Education	Minimum 35 PDUs overall with a minimum of 8 PDUs from Technical, Leadership, and Strategic areas. The remaining 11 can be across any of the PMI Talent Triangle.
# of PDUs in Giving Back	Maximum 25
PDU Transfer to Next Period	Up to 20 PDUs earned in the final 12 months of the certification cycle
Additional Remark	PMI-PBA PDUs must be specialized in business analysis
When Should You Pursue this Certification?	I believe this is an ideal certification for professionals who want to demonstrate their ability to analyze business problems and solution

	requirements. Pursue this once you fulfill the basic qualifications.
URL for Handbook	http://www.pmi.org/~/media/PDF/ Certifications/PMI-PBA- Handbook.ashx

At the time this book is being written, there are slightly fewer than 300 certified PMI-PBAs. But this is growing rapidly from 182 certified PMI-PBAs in December 2014 to about 234 in March 2015, a growth of 56% in a span of roughly 4 months.

I believe you should be interested in this certification for three reasons: 1) based on my research of major job sites like Monster.com, there are more business analyst jobs; 2) it differentiates you from other candidates; and 3) skill-building. In all my years of experience, for every one project manager on a complex project, there are at least two to three business analysts. Thus, I was not surprised to find more jobs for business analysts. Having the PMI-PBA certification also gives you an edge in the competitive job market. Also, this is a rare opportunity to get in on the ground floor of a growing certification. But perhaps the most important reason is skill-building. PMI-PBA represents a core set of business skills that are invaluable to business professionals as they grow and mature. The abilities to understand and critically analyze business requirements, manage stakeholders, align strategies, and tackle change are essential skills for all business professionals.

vi. PMI Agile Certified Practitioner (PMI-ACP)

In software development, agile methodology has been steadily gaining popularity over the past two decades. Starting with Dynamic System Development Methodology (DSDM) in 1994 to the latest developments in extreme programming, the philosophy of agile is to address one fundamental problem in complex projects: people often do not know what they want. A lack of precision in requirements and customers changing their minds are the most common problems plaguing complex projects, especially in software development. In traditional project management methodology, also known as the waterfall approach, changes to a project become progressively prohibitive in terms of cost and schedule impact. That being said, to fully conceive of a complex deliverable at the beginning of a project is often unrealistic. Thus, project changes are frequent and often painful for the project team. Agile methods break down large and often long project courses into shorter and incremental sprints. This way, changes can be made more quickly, value can be realized faster, and if there are mistakes or failures, the cost is less prohibitive.

Agile project management, sometimes known as agile management, embraces the incremental, iterative, flexible, and modular approach used in the design and execution of engineering, information technology, and even new product and services development. From a broader perspective, the rise of agile methodology is a reflection of today's competitive landscape. With rising competition comes greater uncertainty.

Agile project management holds the promise of greater agility and flexibility in our ever-changing world.

Table 13: PMI Agile Certified Practitioner (PMI-ACP) Summary

A. Qualifications	
General Project Experience	2,000 hours working on project teams within the last 5 years; active PMP® or PgMP® will satisfy this requirement
Agile Project Experience	1,500 hours working on agile project teams or with agile methodologies within the last 3 years
Additional Requirement	21 hours in agile practices
B. Certification Fees (First Time, Re-Exam, and CCR)	
Exam Fees for CBT (Member/Non-Member)	$435 or €365 / $495 or €415
Re-Exam Fees for CBT (Member/Non-Member)	$335 or €280 / $335 or €330
CCR Renewal (Member/Non-Member)	$60 / $150

C. Certification Exam	
# of Questions (Scored / Pre-Test/ Total)	100 / 20 / 120
Allocated Time for Exam in Hours	3
Approx. Time per Question in Seconds	90
Language Aid	1
D. Continual Certification Requirement	
Certification Period in Years	3
Total # of PDUs	30
# of PDUs in Education	Minimum 18 PDUs overall with a minimum of 4 PDUs from Technical, Leadership, and Strategic areas. The remaining 6 can be across any of the PMI Talent Triangle.
# of PDUs in Giving Back	Maximum 12
PDU Transfer to Next Period	Up to 10 PDUs earned in the final 12 months of the certification cycle
Additional Remark	PMI-ACP PDUs must be specialized in agile project management
When Should You Pursue this Certification?	I believe this certification nicely complements PMP, PgMP, and

	even CAPM. Pursue this if you work in a fast paced industry.
URL for Handbook	http://www.pmi.org/en/Certificati on/~/media/PDF/Certifications/PM I-ACP_Handbook.ashx

The popularity of agile project management is reflected in the rapid growth of PMI-ACP credential holders. In the first year it was introduced, there were 1,611 PMI-ACP professionals by December 2012. By March 2015, there were 7,528, a growth of over 350% in less than 3 years.

In investigating the reasons why agile project management has grown so swiftly, I randomly examined select data from a variety of sources. I estimate that approximately 70% of the PMI-ACP credential holders also have another PMI certification. While this can be interpreted in a number of ways, the most likely reason is that PMI-ACP is a powerful complement to the Project Management Profession (PMP). The PMI-ACP qualification requirement supports this prediction, as the requirement indicates 2,000 hours of experience on project teams in addition to the 1,500 hours required on agile projects.

vii. PMI Risk Management Professional (PMI-RMP)

Projects are designed to change the status quo of an organization, and for that reason they are inherently risky. In an environment in which the only constant is change, project professionals must confront risks boldly yet carefully. Project risk management professionals are part of the solution to managing increasingly complex and unpredictable environments. By identifying, evaluating, and managing risk, risk management is becoming an integral part of large projects.

Table 14: PMI Risk Management Professional (PMI-RMP) Summary

A. Qualifications	
Secondary Degree	4,500 hours of project risk management experience + 40 hours of project risk management education
Advanced Degree	3,000 hours of project risk management experience + 30 hours of project risk management education
B. Certification Fees (First Time, Re-Exam, and CCR)	
Exam Fees for CBT (Member/Non-Member)	$520 or €430 / $670 or €555
Re-Exam Fees for CBT (Member/Non-Member)	$335 or €280 / $435 or €365
CCR Renewal (Member/Non-Member)	$60 / $150

C. Certification Exam	
# of Questions (Scored / Pre-Test/ Total)	150 / 20 / 170
Allocated Time for Exam in Hours	3.5
Approx. Time per Question in Seconds	74.1
Language Aid	1
D. Continual Certification Requirement	
Certification Period in Years	3
Total # of PDUs	30
# of PDUs in Education	Minimum 18 PDUs overall with a minimum of 4 PDUs from Technical, Leadership, and Strategic areas. The remaining 6 can be across any of the PMI Talent Triangle.
# of PDUs in Giving Back	Maximum 12
PDU Transfer to Next Period	Up to 10 PDUs earned in the final 12 months of the certification cycle
Additional Remark	PMI-RMP PDUs must be specialized in project risk management
When Should You Pursue this Certification?	Risk management is a specialized area, but in my experience, managing risk well is a sign of true project management expertise. My suggestion

	is to pursue this certification as a complementary certification to PMP, PgMP, and/or PfMP. If you desire to pursue this independently, you should do so once you fulfill the stated qualifications.
URL for Handbook	http://www.pmi.org/Certification/~/media/PDF/Certifications/PMI-RMP_Handbook.ashx

Since its inception, PMI-RMP has been growing healthy at about an annual growth rate of about 52%. While the growth rate has cooled somewhat in recent years as the pool of credential holders increased, it remains strong. Risk management, especially with respect to specialized areas such as data confidentiality, privacy, and financial risk management, are often headline news around the world. This combined with the escalating complexity of projects will fuel this certification for years to come.

viii. PMI Scheduling Professional (PMI-SP)

Project professionals work closely with time management and schedules. As a specialty area of focus, project scheduling professionals focus on developing and maintaining large and complex schedules such as those required for projects in construction, military, and large-scale industrial projects. These project schedules can be composed of thousands of lines of tasks whose management demands high-level competency,

Table 15: PMI Scheduling Professional (PMISP) Summary

A. Qualifications	
Secondary Degree	5,000 hours of project scheduling experience + 40 hours of project scheduling education
Advanced Degree	3,500 hours of project scheduling experience + 30 hours of project scheduling education
B. Certification Fees (First Time, Re-Exam, and CCR)	
Exam Fees for CBT (Member/Non-Member)	$520 or €430 / $670 or €555
Re-Exam Fees for CBT (Member/Non-Member)	$335 or €280 / $435 or €365
CCR Renewal (Member/Non-Member)	$60 / $150
C. Certification Exam	
# of Questions (Scored / Pre-Test/ Total)	150 / 20 / 170
Allocated Time for Exam in Hours	3.5
Approx. Time per Question in Seconds	74.1

Language Aid	1
D. Continual Certification Requirement	
Certification Period in Years	3
Total # of PDUs	30
# of PDUs in Education	Minimum 18 PDUs overall with a minimum of 4 PDUs from Technical, Leadership, and Strategic areas. The remaining 6 can be across any of the PMI Talent Triangle.
# of PDUs in Giving Back	Maximum 12
PDU Transfer to Next Period	Up to 10 PDUs earned in the final 12 months of the certification cycle
Additional Remark	PMI-SP PDUs must be specialized in project schedule
When Should You Pursue this Certification?	Scheduling is both a core and specialized area. Project professionals should be very comfortable with scheduling in general. But if you work in an industry where large, long, and complex projects are the norm, the PMI-SP would give you an extra edge that demonstrates your capacity for developing complex schedules and managing their interdependencies and costs.

URL for Handbook	http://www.pmi.org/Certification/~ /media/PDF/Certifications/PMI- SP_Handbook.ashx

Even though PMI-SP growth is modest when compared to PMI-RMP, it still clocks in at a healthy 33% average annual rate of growth. This enforces the idea that scheduling is often viewed as a core component of project management. In select industries such as defense, construction, and public works, large and complicated project schedules are the norm. It is in situations such as these that scheduling professionals shine, while developing specialty skills to coordinate and manage large numbers of tasks with interdependencies makes them indispensable project managers.

B. What do you need to do to maintain certifications?

In late 2015, PMI announced the shift to the new PMI Talent Triangle™ model that is based on PMI's research of contemporary business needs. The effective date for the new model is January 2016.

Professional Development Units (PDUs) are awarded in two broad categories: Education and Giving Back to the Profession. Education contains three categories of skill sets: technical project management, leadership, and strategic and business management. Generally, there are five ways to learn and earn PDUs:

1. Courses or Training, especially by PMI Registered Education Providers (R.E.P.)
2. Organizational Meetings (e.g. Chapter Meetings)
3. Self-paced learning through online or digital media
4. Self-directed reading
5. Informal learning through interaction with others

Giving back to the profession are activities contributing to the vitality of the profession. This includes volunteering, creating new knowledge and content, giving a presentation, sharing knowledge and working as a practitioner. Specifically on working as a practitioner, there is a maximum of 8 PDUs per cycle for PMP, PgMP, PfMP, and PMI-PBA and a maximum of 4 PDUs per cycle for PMI-ACP, PMI-RMP, and PMI-SP.

Generally, you earn one PDU per hour of effort. If you earn more PDUs than required for a period, you can transfer a portion to the next period. Only PDUs earned within the 12 months of the certification cycle can be applied to the next cycle.

Since this is new (at the time of publishing this book), PMI may release updated information. For more information on Continuing Certification Requirements (CCRS), download the CCR Handbook here:

http://www.pmi.org/~/media/PDF/Certifications/handbooks/ccr-certification-requirements-handbook.ashx.

C. Are there other project management standards and certifications?

PMI is not the only professional project management organization, but it is the most influential and its certifications are the most recognized in the world, especially in the Americas. If you are interested in exploring other organizations, I recommend examining the International Project Management Association (IPMA) at http://ipma.ch. IPMA is an international umbrella organization for national project management associations in over 57 countries with over 120,000 members as of 2012.[xvi]

Another organization worth mentioning is AXELOS Ltd, a joint venture between the HM Cabinet Office and Capita plc. AXELOS owns a popular project management methodology called Projects IN Controlled Environments, commonly known as PRINCE2®. This certification was initially developed by the United Kingdom's Central Computer and Telecommunications Agency. PRINCE2 gained popularity in the mid-1990s, and not only among information technology professionals. Today, it is the de facto standard methodology for project management in the United Kingdom and across much of Europe. In addition to PRINCE2, AXELOS offers a more advanced certification for program managers called Managing Successful Programmes (MSP®) and MoP® or Management of Portfolios for portfolio management. Recently, in June 2015, AXELOS started offering PRINCE2 Agile to promote greater flexibility and adaptability in project management processes. Think of it this way PRINCE2 is to PMP as MSP is to PgMP.

CompTIA also offers CompTIA's Project+, which is a more entry-level project management certification designed for information technology specialists. The certification is similar to PMI's CAPM.

Both of these certifications are more widely recognized in Europe. However, a full coverage of their significant merits is beyond the scope of this book and may be explored in the future.

4. Project Management Career Ladder

"The biggest mistake that you can make is to believe that you are working for somebody else. Job security is gone. The driving force of a career must come from the individual. Remember: Jobs are owned by the company, you own your career!"

Earl Nightingale

When it comes to the project management career ladder, there is no one standard across the industry. Project intensity varies greatly from one business environment to another. Some organizations are more operationally focused, with few or occasional projects. This tends to be true of mature industries where change is minimal. For example, in a consumer manufacturing plant, the bulk of the work in a plant is often focused on producing the goods and services for the market. There are projects to be sure, whether that be improving an existing production line or expanding a plant, but the majority of the work is operational. Other sectors – usually in high tech or turbulent industries where change is the norm – are very project-intensive. Even across companies in the same industry, the level of project intensity can vary greatly.

There are many variables that determine project intensity, but I believe the top four factors to be 1) size, 2) complicatedness, 3) complexity, and 4) number of simultaneous projects. Larger projects naturally require more resources and thus put greater pressure on an organization. Complicatedness refers to the number of interrelated components or parties involved. For example, a project within one department is typically less complicated than an inter-departmental project. Complexity refers to the degree of unpredictability and uncertainty that can occur on projects. This frequently occurs in rapidly evolving sectors such as information systems or advanced fields of science or engineering in which risky projects live on the "bleeding edge" of technology. Perhaps the most obvious factor contributing to project intensity is the number of projects being attempted simultaneously. Usually, the more projects an organization undertakes at the same time, the greater the level of organizational stress.

A few additional factors can influence project intensity and can bear even more impact than size, complexity, uncertainty, and number. Diversity, while widely celebrated among organizations, can contribute to conflicts within organizations. When properly managed, greater diversity, which correlates with greater conflicts, can challenge the status quo and produce superior results in the long run. After all, organizations that foster a healthy degree of conflict can avoid managerial problems such as groupthink, low energy, and stale ideas. But when diversity is poorly managed, it can lead to ineffective project environments in which the voice of the minority is suppressed. Organizational politics can also play a strong role in shaping the project environment. Politics exist in all organizations when decisions are not based on merits but rather self-interest. Political power play is real, and its impact can be both positive and negative, depending on whose perspective is considered. A final factor worth mentioning is organizational culture. Some firms develop a healthy "execution mindset" which encourages employees at all levels to make decisions, take risks, tackle problems, and strive toward progress efficiently and effectively. Other organizations move slowly and easily succumb to inertia.

Against this backdrop, project professionals perform their work. This sliding scale of project intensity dispenses a great variety of project management career paths. As a management consultant who has worked for many organizations across a wide range of industries and sectors including financial services, telecommunications, consumer products, software industry, non-profits, and professional services, I have witnessed many models of project management career paths. The model presented in this book is built mainly on the business consulting trajectory of project management. I believe it is a more universally applicable model and its progressions are logically consistent. Certain industries have specialized project management roles such as expeditors, schedulers, and estimators. The career ladder in this book mainly reflects ever increasing responsibilities and job titles. As you read this chapter, keep in mind that, depending on your organization and industry, your career path is likely to deviate in some or many respects. Thus, you will need to customize your own conceptual ladder.

This chapter attempts to address these questions:

A. What does a project management career ladder look like?
B. What are the core skills required to be an effective project manager?
C. How do these skills map to the career ladder?
D. Are there core skills and qualification guidelines?

A. What does a project management career ladder look like?

There are many potential roles and responsibilities in project management. For the sake of simplicity and the ease of discussion, I have here grouped them into three stages of professional growth:

Table 16: Three Stages of Professional Growth

Stage	Description
Entry-Level	Broadly speaking, entry-level refers to people who have little or no hands-on experience in project management. Their amount of knowledge varies. At the entry level, the expected standard of performance, especially when acting independently, is gentle. As an entry-level professional, your goal should be to experience and learn under the guidance of more senior project professionals.
Skilled Project Managers	Skilled project managers should be able to independently manage small, medium, and sometimes large and complex projects. In addition to possessing a significant amount of project management knowledge, they should also be able to make sound business judgements as is often required on projects. At this level, skilled project managers should be looking to expand their capabilities of managing

Stage	Description
	projects with greater scale and complexity. Their primary focus should be on key project success criteria and delivery results that meet expectations.
Expert Project Manager	Expert project managers are seasoned professionals who can handle most project situations. Often, they have gone beyond the realm of projects and perhaps even programs. At the most senior level, expert project managers have become drivers or facilitators to key project investment decisions at a portfolio level. Expert project managers are the "go-to" people in organizations and inevitably work on some of the most challenging and perplexing problems related to projects. Expert project managers do not necessarily become portfolio managers, depending on an organization's needs and their own interests. As a Trekkie, I am reminded of *Star Trek 4: The Voyage Home*, when Captain Kirk prefers to be a captain who is project-managing his own ship rather than being an admiral who sits in the corner office examining portfolios of projects from afar. This analogy applies well here. Even in my career, I have given up the equivalent of an "admiralty" and became the "captain" of a large program.

Within each stage of the profession, there can be multiple roles, with a general progression toward increasing responsibilities and accountabilities.

Figure 4: Conceptual Project Management Career Ladder

Figure 4: Conceptual Project Management Career Ladder

Project Executive

Skilled Project Manager

Entry Level

Portfolio Manager / Director

Program Director

Sr. Project or Program Manager

Project Manager

Jr. Project Manager

Project Analyst

Project Assistant

Accountabilities

Time

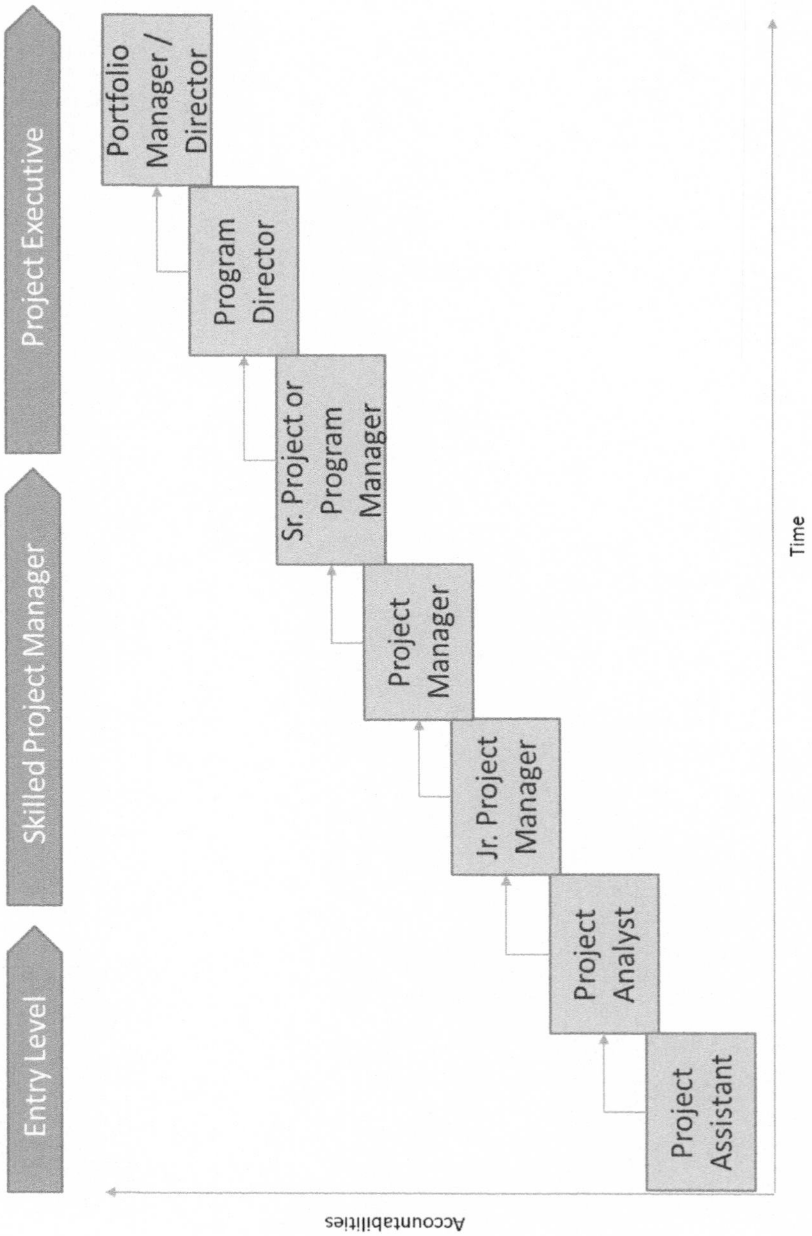

Table 17 below outlines seven common project management career steps, roughly mapped to the three stages of professional growth.

Table 17: Seven Common Steps in the Project Management Career Ladder

Steps	Description
Entry Level	
Project Assistant	This is an entry-level position which leads into a career in project management. As a project assistant, the individual will support project managers on a variety of project management duties. These include: meeting logistics and minutes, coordinating resources, managing action items, conducting preliminary research, securing documents, and helping manage resources.
Project Analyst	As project analyst, this individual will provide analytical support to project and program managers. In addition, the project analyst will be responsible for certain sub-processes and perhaps even manage an entire process such as change requests, configuration management, or project tracking. This position can also support project and program managers in terms of meeting logistics, meeting minutes, preparing portfolio management and resource discussions, and documentation support.

Steps	Description
Skilled Project Managers	
Junior Project Manager	As junior project manager, the individual will be fully responsible for managing small to moderate projects and specified deliverables. Working with the leads from other project tracks and/or other project managers, the junior project manager will have full budgeting and resource responsibilities for their projects. In addition, he/she will be fully accountable for the completion of the project. The expectation is that the junior project manager will be able to operate independently and effectively manage expectations and drive small to moderate projects to completion.
Project Manager	As project manager, the individual will be fully responsible for managing moderate to select large projects. Working with a functional or track lead and/or other project managers, the project manager will have full budgeting and resource responsibilities for their projects. In addition, he/she will be fully accountable for the completion of the project. The expectation is that the project manager will be able to operate independently and effectively manage expectations and drive moderate to larger projects to completion.
Senior Project / Program Manager	As senior project manager or program manager, the individual will be fully responsible for managing large projects and programs. Working with the sponsor, the senior project manager will have full budgeting and resource responsibilities for the project. In addition,

Steps	Description
	he/she will be fully accountable for the completion of the project and program.
Expert Project Managers	
Program Director	As program director, the individual will be working on programs that are composed of multiple projects or large, independent projects. In addition to the tasks mentioned under project manager, he/she will be responsible for executive communication, methodology development / enhancement, and building / enriching a center of knowledge exchange.
Portfolio Manager / Director	As portfolio manager / director, this individual will work to align a collection or portfolio of projects and programs with the business strategy. Accountability is associated with delivering business value within acceptable risks and costs. He/she will be responsible for achieving consistent and sustainable project excellence and developing key people. Furthermore, portfolio managers / directors are accountable for aligning business strategy and execution.

In addition to these seven common roles, there are many additional roles and titles depending upon the industry and organization.

Figure 5: Additional Project Management Titles

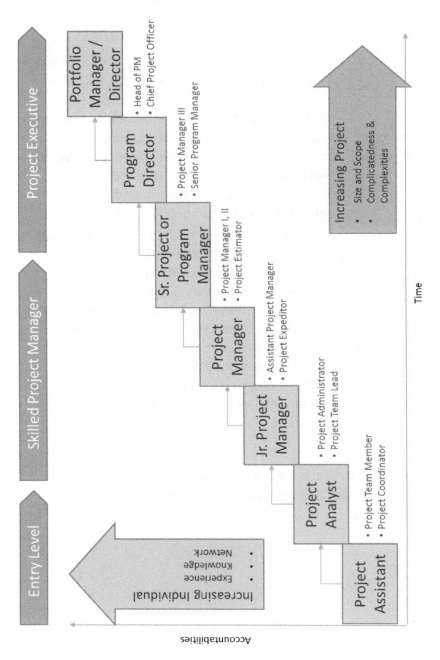

Figure 5 presents twelve additional titles mapped approximately to the seven roles. As shown in the figure, as project professionals grow in experience, knowledge, network, and skills, they assume increasing responsibilities for managing projects of greater size, scope, complexity, and uncertainty.

B. What are the core skills required to be an effective project manager?

Based on my more than twenty years of experience working with Global and Fortune 500 clients as well as leading non-profit organizations across multiple industries such as telecommunication, financial services, pharmaceutical, education, and consumer products, I believe effective project managers must have a broad range of skills across multiple disciplines. The following framework organizes effective project management skills into four dimensions:

A. General Business Skills: These are universal business management skills required for all business professionals.

B. Discipline-Specific Skills: These are the specific skills within each of the project management disciplines including project, program, portfolio, risk, and schedule management as well as business analysis.

C. Organizational Skills: In addition to general business and discipline-specific skills, successful project managers must also possess the skills needed to build teams and lead organizations. This is especially important in intense project environments where the

    soft skills of managing organizational change often
    trump the hard skills of creating complex schedules.

D. Desirable Attitude, Behavior, and Personal Traits: In
    addition to skills, an effective project professional must
    also possess strong character and attitude.

In the following sections, I will present my views on a select number of skills, characteristics, and traits. This list encompasses the skills, characteristics, and traits that I consider to be high-priority, and is not designed to be exhaustive.

i. General Business Skills

Project management is a microcosm of business management. Therefore, most management skills are directly applicable to project management. To understand the key difference, let's return to the pressure cooker analogy. Project management functions in a stressful, high-pressure environment in which schedule and delivery are paramount with the stress of schedule and delivery.

Naturally, there are many necessary skills at this level. The table below lists twelve general business skills that are most relevant to project management.

Table 18: General Business Skills

Name	Description
Communication	A project manager must effectively exchange ideas, views, and directives, either orally or in written form, that serve as the basis for collaboration.
Engagement Management	A project manager should utilize a more strategic mindset when managing work and relationships. In addition to focus on tasks, also consider the broader implications of the work.
General Business Knowledge	An effective project manager knows that projects are constantly influenced by fluctuating environments, and therefore he/she must be constantly updating his/her general business knowledge, such as the latest developments in project management.
Information Management / Sharing	Since a project manager often functions as a coach or mentor to junior team members and other project managers, he or she should possess a desire to learn, organize data and information, and share this with others.
Leadership	A project manager must take responsibility for his or her actions and effectively set directions for his or her teams.
Organizational Savvy	A project manager must be competent in understanding how organizations work and utilizing that knowledge to more effectively navigate organizational obstacles.

Name	Description
Personal Relationships	A project manager must be able to work well with others, build positive connections, and develop trusting relationships.
Product & Service Knowledge	A project manager must become intimately familiar with his or her organization's products and services so that he or she can develop the most effective perspective and context for managing projects.
Project Management (General)	Since project management consists of both specific and general knowledge sets, a project manager must be able to manage time, budget, scope, and resources.
Project Management Process	A project manager must understand and utilize project management processes and workflows to ensure greater consistency and repeatability in project execution.
Research & Analysis	When confronted with competing choices, a project manager must be able to conduct research, including finding, documenting, analyzing, and prioritizing the findings.
Teamwork	A project manager must understand that a project's success requires more than him/herself, and therefore must be able to develop and harness high-performing teams.

ii. Discipline-Specific Skills

In addition to general business knowledge, project professionals must possess a strong set of discipline-specific knowledge and skills. Below is a list of nine discipline-specific skills and the roles to which they play.

Table 19: Project, Program, and Portfolio Management Discipline-Specific Skills

Name	Description
Project Management - Specialized Knowledge Areas	The ability to comprehend and apply a standard body of project management knowledge. Note: this set of specialized skills is different from the general business skills listed above; there, project management skills are applied generally, and here, the skills are more in-depth, systemized, and specialized; for example, most professionals can manage risk and create checklists, but the knowledge and skills necessary to develop comprehensive project plans fall into this category.
Program / Portfolio Management - Operating	The ability of a project professional to perform the required work in a program and/or portfolio management environment.
Program Management - Establishing & Leading	The ability to establish and lead programs in a program management environment.

Name	Description
Portfolio Management - Establishing & Leading	The ability to establish, manage, and administer project portfolio functions that connect business strategy with implementation.
Business Process Design	The ability to design, modify, and improve business processes that are germane to projects; specialty skills are required to identify, analyze, recommend, and implement change for process improvements.
Business Analysis	The ability to identify, analyze, evaluate, document, and communicate business requirements for project implementation.
Execution Planning & Management	The ability to bridge strategy formulation with execution and implementation, which includes aligning strategy with projects, analyzing organizational change readiness, and managing capability and capacity.
Managing Implementation Vendors	The aptitude for developing relationships with external vendors into mutually beneficial alliances.
Product Management	The ability to develop, plan, forecast, produce, market, and maintain products and services throughout the project lifecycle.

iii. Organizational Skills

Macro-organizational trends are diverging in interesting ways as more work is being done on the one hand by individual freelancers and on the other hand by large, complicated, mega-merged organizations. The rise in popularity of these two trends is not necessarily a paradox. Organizations come together when executives see it as strategic in terms of synergy, economy of scale or scope, or market domination. Freelance labor, conversely, is done by non-employees, but freelancing also allows for greater flexibility and maneuverability. Why is this important for the project management profession? Two reasons:

- These two trends yield very different work environments, and it is up to project professionals to develop the necessary organizational skills to navigate today's changing business environments.
- Intense project environments require greater awareness and a more robust skill set to create centralized teams and functions for managing projects. This is particularly important within organizations striving toward consistency, predictability, and repeatability of project success while alleviating shortcomings and deficiencies.

This trend toward the centralization of project management activities has fueled the growth of the project, program, and portfolio management office – a centralized team for managing projects. This team goes by many names, including PMO, Center of Excellence, Competency Center, Project

Services, and Management Services. Because it's the most popular, I will refer to this centralized team as PMO.

The skills required to manage a PMO are vast, and it is beyond the goal of this book to cover them comprehensively. Rather, I will pinpoint four skill sets that I believe are the most important.

Table 20: Project Organization Skills

Name	Description
Human Development	The ability to develop people in an organization with intense projects; project managers are leaders and influencers, and one of the ten knowledge areas in PMBOK is related to motivating and growing people.
Methodological Development	The ability to create and refine organizational project management methodologies to ensure consistency of delivery across the organization; this is significantly more challenging than executing standalone projects, and requires systematic and processed thinking.
Cultural Change	The ability to carefully manage change, both subtle and wholesale, as an organization evolves.
Knowledge Management	The ability to manage knowledge, which is one of the most important assets of any organization; project managers are often at the forefront of creating new

Name	Description
	knowledge through project execution and lessons learned.

iv. Behavior & Attitudes

Project managers are leaders by virtue of what they do. There are many studies on leadership qualities, but I've distilled three aspects of leadership that are essential for project management:

- A project manager must have a strong character so that he or she can be a beacon of consistency amidst a sea of changes and challenges on projects.
- A project manager must have the right attitude, so that he or she is able to successfully confront problems.
- A project manager must embrace the organizational culture to guide his or her behavior and mindset to achieve sustained success for his or her organization.

The table below provides a list of the key character, attitude, and cultural characteristics that I believe are essential for project managers.

Table 21: Soft Skills: Attitude, Behavior, and Culture

Name	Description
Attitude	<ul><li>Appreciative</li><li>Communicates proactively and honestly</li><li>Confident, but not overbearing</li><li>Assertive, but not overly-aggressive</li><li>Flexible with schedule and approach</li><li>Helpful</li><li>Pleasant and upbeat</li><li>Willing to go the extra mile</li></ul>
Behavior	<ul><li>Always seeks opportunities to improve oneself and the department</li><li>Applies oneself to solving tough problems</li><li>Goes the extra mile to understand things from another's perspective</li><li>Reacts constructively to change and evolution</li><li>Seeks feedback and assistance when required</li><li>Receives feedback constructively</li><li>Always remains as objective as possible</li><li>Works constructively even when outside one's comfort zone</li></ul>
Cultural Characteristics	<ul><li>Prioritizes the general (company) interest or department interest over individual interest</li><li>Prioritizes doing the right thing above other concerns</li><li>Eager to consult with and help others within the company</li></ul>

Name	Description
	• Rigorously applies implementation processes
	• Flexible with approaches, processes, methods, and tools
	• Clearly defines authority, accountability, and responsibility (in this order) on all assignments
	• Promotes collaboration, teamwork, and shared accountability
	• Encourages company to embrace positive change
	• Has fun and enjoys the work

C. How do these skills map to the career ladder?

In this section, I will go into more details about the skill sets that I've already laid out, and how these skills play out at each level of project management. Since the skills are largely the same for both positions, I've combined the Program Director and Portfolio Manager skills. The major difference between Portfolio Managers and Program Directors has to do with scope of responsibilities and visibility, as Portfolio Managers often sit at a higher level within their organization.

It is important to remember, as the career ladder in "Figure 4: Conceptual Project Management Career Ladder" illustrates that skill sets are cumulative – in other words, the skills required for a more advanced position also consist of the skills gleaned from the preceding position. Though in real life there is some nuance and complexity to this, it is useful to remember from a skill-building perspective.

i. General Business Skills - Communication

Table 22: General Business Skills – Communication Skills

Level	Description
Project Assistant	<ul><li>Actively participates in project meetings</li><li>Answers questions directly and concisely</li></ul>
Project Analyst	<ul><li>Communicates easily and effectively with team members</li><li>Writes brief and concise emails</li></ul>
Jr. Project Manager	<ul><li>Leads project meetings</li><li>Communicates effectively with team members and stakeholders</li><li>Facilitates meetings and drives the team towards achieving its objectives</li><li>Listens actively, processes inputs, and provides proper feedback</li><li>Summarizes and communicates key points</li></ul>
Project Manager	<ul><li>Leads executive meetings</li><li>Communicates orally in an executive summary fashion</li><li>Communicates easily and effectively with client managers</li><li>Understands when it is most effective to speak or provide input</li></ul>
Senior Project /	<ul><li>Communicates with busy executives in a concise and articulate fashion</li></ul>

Level	Description
Program Manager	• Adapts communication style to other participants / clients • Utilizes crisp, straightforward language as opposed to jargon, "consulting-speak," or obscure language
Program Director	• Serves as a strong leadership presence in all program meetings

ii. General Business Skills – Engagement Management

Table 23: General Business Skills – Engagement Management

Level	Description
Project Assistant	• Clearly understands internal client needs • Manages time effectively
Project Analyst	• Identifies and analyzes issues within the project team • Provides data-driven analyses of issues and conflicts within the project team • Recommends ways to deal with problems and issues • Delegates tasks and responsibilities to project team members and clients
Jr. Project Manager	• Identifies, analyzes, mitigates, and resolves conflicts within projects • Clearly articulates internal client needs to project team and other executives • Manages difficult people

Level	Description
	• Identifies and addresses scope change • Simultaneously leads multiple smaller projects or engagements • Develops comprehensive work plans and budgets • Manages project budgets and reports potential budget issues to track leads and/or project sponsors
Project Manager	• Proactively identifies, analyzes, mitigates, and resolves conflicts within projects • Articulates client expectations and manages them accordingly • Effectively manages difficult and evolving situations • Identifies and addresses scope change • Simultaneously leads multiple moderately-sized engagements • Skillfully delegates tasks and responsibilities to project team members and clients • Manages project budgets and proactively reports potential budget issues to key stakeholders, escalating issues when necessary
Senior Project / Program Manager	• Identifies and addresses client-side obstacles • Corrals resources to meet client expectations • Clearly articulates internal client needs, opportunities, and challenges to clients and other executives

Level	Description
	• Involves and provides communication to the leadership team as appropriate • Properly confronts internal clients as necessary • Effectively leads larger engagements
Program Director	• Effectively removes obstacles • Resolves high-level engagement issues with project sponsors • Accurately and completely provides reports at project health meetings and program/project status meetings • Proactively leads and manages engagements • Navigates challenging and evolving client situations, such as key personnel shifts, management disagreements, and competition • Simultaneously manages multiple, complex client engagements, such as overseeing multiple project managers

iii. General Business Skills – General Business Knowledge

Table 24: General Business Skills – General Business Knowledge

Level	Description
Project Assistant	• Regularly consumes one or more of the general business publications • Understands and consistently applies common business and technical vocabulary
Project Analyst	• Frequently reads firm publications • Generally grasps external market trends
Jr. Project Manager	• Regularly consumes one or more of the specialized publications relevant to project management and technology • Generally understands the key competitor positions within an industry
Project Manager	• Participates in industry seminars and meetings • Generally understands the rules and regulations, both US and Global, that affect business
Senior Project / Program Manager	• Proactively participates in industry seminars and meetings to advance collective business knowledge
Program Director	• Potentially leads select discussions as a thought-leader

iv. General Business Skills – Information Management & Sharing

Table 25: General Business Skills – Information Management & Sharing

Level	Description
Project Assistant	• Understands the importance of sharing knowledge • Demonstrates willingness to share knowledge
Project Analyst	• Actively shares knowledge, such as project management methods and best practices, with the project team • Coaches project assistants and actively helps improve their understanding
Jr. Project Manager	• Actively works with project teams to collect and share knowledge of program/project management • Coaches project assistants and analysts in all aspects of project management
Project Manager	• Actively works with other project managers to collaborate on project processes, methods, templates, and tools • Coaches junior project managers on all aspects of project management
Senior Project / Program Manager	• Actively shares experiences and knowledge with all members of the department • Actively collects and contributes to knowledge capital

Level	Description
Program Director	• Leads knowledge sharing forums to advance knowledge capital • Develops and enhances approaches, methods and tools to improve implementation processes

v. General Business Skills - Leadership

Table 26: General Business Skills – Leadership

Level	Description
Project Assistant	• Takes responsibility for own actions
Project Analyst	• Understands organizational policies and methodologies • Communicates openly, directly, and frequently • Knows when to offer help or assistance
Jr. Project Manager	• Contributes to project decisions in a constructive, objective, team-oriented way • Exhibits trustworthiness and integrity • Weighs in effectively and constructively on management issues and decisions
Project Manager	• Leads internal initiatives to continuously improve management services • Exhibits accountability and ownership for the success of projects

Level	Description
Senior Project / Program Manager	• Strives to be accessible and approachable • Contributes positively to planning sessions • Prepares management materials and reports in a timely and complete fashion
Program Director	• Takes ultimate responsibility for the success of a program • Reports program activities fully and accurately • Works in the best interest of the department and/or the company

vi. General Business Skills – Organizational Savvy

Table 27: General Business Skills – Organizational Savvy

Level	Description
Project Assistant	• Understands how his or her organization works
Project Analyst	• Effectively works within the culture of his or her organization
Jr. Project Manager	• Sensitively aware of how people and teams function • Assesses the political climate • Identifies organizational issues and problems
Project Manager	• Sensitively aware of how organizations perceive situations and issues

Level	Description
	• Develops a perspective on the political climate • Proactively identifies organizational issues and problems and suggests ways to mitigate risk
Senior Project / Program Manager	• Assesses organizational needs due to changes in technology, process, and/or people • Anticipates land mines and approaches them accordingly
Program Director	• Effectively maneuvers complex political situations

vii. General Business Skills – Personal Relationships

Table 28: General Business Skills – Personal Relationships

Level	Description
Project Assistant	• Establishes trust among project team members
Project Analyst	• Establishes trust among project team members and project manager • Advises project team members on key project trends and metrics
Jr. Project Manager	• Establishes trust among track leads and project team members • Provides analytical advice to project track leads and key stakeholders

Level	Description
Project Manager	• Establishes trust among project team managers
Senior Project / Program Manager	• Establishes trust among project sponsors and other executives • Identifies opportunities to add value
Program Director	• Maintains a strong presence within the project at multiple levels throughout its entirety • Develops opportunities for follow-up or incremental work

viii. General Business Skills – Product & Service Knowledge

Table 29: General Business Skills – Product & Service Knowledge

Level	Description
Project Assistant	• Understands the firm's mission, vision, and value • Understands the firm's objectives
Project Analyst	• Understands the role and service offerings of the organization • Awareness of the major products and their functions
Jr. Project Manager	• Articulates internal processes for demand generation and fulfillment

Level	Description
	• Aware of functions of various departments such as: - Finance - Continuous Improvement - Infrastructure Services - Development - Quality Assurance - Deployment - Support
Project Manager	• Understands the inner-workings of project finance, including project forecasting and resource management
Senior Project / Program Manager	• Understands the target organization and its product/service needs
Program Director	• Possesses a working knowledge of other IT organizations along with an awareness of how to work effectively with them

ix. General Business Skills – Project Management

Table 30: General Business Skills – Project Management

Level	Description
Project Assistant	<ul><li>Provides support for meetings, such as setting up equipment</li><li>Maintains schedule and completes tasks on time</li><li>Completes timesheets in a timely fashion</li><li>Recommends ways to motivate the team</li></ul>
Project Analyst	<ul><li>Crisply and effectively initiates meetings</li><li>Creates useful meeting notes</li><li>Creates and communicates detailed status reports</li><li>Prioritizes activities and makes tradeoffs</li><li>Raises issues and concerns to the project manager appropriately</li><li>Identifies project-level risks and reports these to the project manager</li></ul>
Jr. Project Manager	<ul><li>Identifies the need for group meetings and also the necessary participants</li><li>Manages meetings effectively, ensuring that objectives are met, and action items are identified</li><li>Communicates status to management</li><li>Plans tasks required to complete engagement</li><li>Creates appropriate project plans</li><li>Manages budgets and tracks costs</li></ul>

Level	Description
	• Anticipates risks and proactively mitigates risks by working with client team members • Estimates resource requirements and tasks • Communicates project-specific development needs to the appropriate supervisor
Project Manager	• Identifies escalation points and knows the effective channels of escalation • Proactively facilitates meetings and takes charge when meetings fail to produce results • Communicates status at multiples points to various stakeholders • Plans tasks and interdependencies required to satisfactorily complete a project while preventing issues on other projects • Creates appropriate project plans for different audiences, both executives and team members • Manages project budgets and reports potential budget issues to senior project management and project sponsor • Develops project team members • Fully manages projects with minimal supervision
Senior Project / Program Manager	• Earns the respect of team members • Works with client executives to mitigate high-level risks • Creates executive status reports

Level	Description
	• Motivates and manages all team members effectively • Overcomes obstacles and identifies workarounds • Develops engagement budgets
Program Director	• Conducts high-level meetings with program stakeholders and executives • Motivates program team, especially when morale is low

x. General Business Skills –Project Management Process

Table 31: General Business Skills – Project Management Process

Level	Description
Project Assistant	• Understands the purpose of implementation processes, templates, forms, and tools
Project Analyst	• Appropriately identifies and completes the required processes, tools, templates, and forms • Offers recommendations to continuously improve the processes
Jr. Project Manager	• Determines a working balance between process compliance and project efficiency • Fully abides by implementation processes and makes constructive recommendations to improve the processes

Level	Description
	• Facilitates and potentially owns process change requests (PCRs) to improve implementation processes
Project Manager	• Leverages the continuous improvement process to achieve greater quality, productivity, and superior management of projects • Advocates for process excellence • Owns process change requests (PCRs) to improve implementation processes
Senior Project / Program Manager	• Develops a deeper understanding of the processes and their benefits and challenges in order to find an effective balance on projects • Develops a strong perspective on process improvement and actively works toward improving processes • Proactively leads process change
Program Director	• Acts as a thought-leader on process excellence • Serves as a "go-to " on select process areas • Champions process improvement

xi. General Business Skills –Research & Analysis

Table 32: General Business Skills – Research & Analysis

Level	Description
Project Assistant	• Understands the purpose of the research and analysis
Project Analyst	• Ability to rapidly develop / find case studies and relevant examples • Draws well integrated conclusions/insights from analyses • Has appropriate perspective on trade press and research sources
Jr. Project Manager	• Creates/identifies relevant case studies to support key points of the argument • Assesses business and technology trends • Familiarity with basics of statistics
Project Manager	• Familiarity with industry best practices • Understands the general business needs of the organization and the relevant technology trends • Intermediate knowledge of statistics • Digests 3rd party research into relevant and usable information
Senior Project / Program Manager	• Knowledge of key industry case studies and "Best Practices" • Defines objectives and scope of research efforts • Identifies research subjects/ areas of expertise that the Management Services must develop

Level	Description
Program Director	• Develop best practices to support the organization

xii. General Business Skills –Teamwork

Table 33: General Business Skills – Teamwork

Level	Description
Project Assistant	• Communicates effectively and politely in a team setting • Goes the extra mile if required • Prioritizes the interests of the team
Project Analyst	• Communicates effectively and politely in a team setting • Shares the credit • Takes responsibility • Supports others
Jr. Project Manager	• Knows when to be direct and when to be indirect • Works well with difficult team members • Resolves intra-team conflicts
Project Manager	• Ascertains the appropriate communication style to use in different situations • Actively seek ways to improve collaboration • Clarifies ambiguities and resolves team conflicts

Level	Description
Senior Project / Program Manager	• Provides constructive feedback • Understands and respects others' business needs • Confidently provides input at the appropriate time
Program Director	• Applies organizational development techniques to further develop teams

xiii. Discipline-Specific - Project Management - Specialized Knowledge Areas

Table 34: Discipline-Specific – Project Management – Specialized Knowledge Areas

Level	Description
Project Assistant	• Aware of the key project management knowledge areas
Project Analyst	• Aware of the following project management knowledge areas (PMI) 1. Project Integration Management 2. Scope Management 3. Time Management 4. Cost Management 5. Communications Management 6. Stakeholder Management 7. Risk Management 8. Quality Management 9. HR Management 10. Procurement Management

Level	Description
Jr. Project Manager	• Possess a strong working knowledge of at least the first 5 PMI knowledge areas and 2 of the remaining 5 areas
Project Manager	• Possess a strong working knowledge of at least the first 6 PMI knowledge areas and 2 of the remaining 4 areas
Senior Project / Program Manager	• Possess a strong working knowledge of at least the first 7 PMI knowledge areas and 1 of the remaining 3 areas
Program Director	• Possess a strong working knowledge of all knowledge areas and project management processes

xiv. Discipline-Specific – Program / Portfolio Management (Operating)

Table 35: Discipline-Specific – Program / Portfolio Management (Operating)

Level	Description
Project Assistant	• Administers program/portfolio activities
Project Analyst	• Articulates challenges, benefits, best practices, and client case studies
Jr. Project Manager	• Determines when and why the program or portfolio management structure is more suitable than project management

Level	Description
Project Manager	• Finds and develops new tools to advance an approach and methodology • Manages select program/portfolio processes
Senior Project / Program Manager	• Applies and operates a basic program for moderately sized programs
Program Director	• Operates all types and sizes of programs and/or portfolios • Navigates organizational issues and concerns, to establish the program / portfolio management office • Develops company's program and/or portfolio capabilities

xv. Discipline-Specific – Program Management (Establishing & Leading)

Table 36: Discipline-Specific – Program Management (Establishing and Leading)

Level	Description
Project Assistant	• Understands the basics of establishing program management
Project Analyst	• Understands the business needs of establishing program management
Jr. Project Manager	• Assists others in designing a program approach, along with its structure,

Level	Description
	processes, and tools for small-moderate programs
Project Manager	<ul><li>Assists others in designing a program approach, along with its structure, processes, and tools for moderate-large programs</li><li>Discerns micro vs. macro program risks and appropriately mitigates these risks</li></ul>
Senior Project / Program Manager	<ul><li>Understands the difference between initiative-specific programs and enterprise program management office</li><li>Independently designs and implements initiative-specific programs for moderate-large programs</li></ul>
Program Director	<ul><li>Serves as a thought-leader with respect to program management and/or program management office</li><li>Designs and implements large initiative-specific programs or enterprise programs</li></ul>

xvi. Discipline-Specific – Portfolio Management (Establishing & Leading)

Table 37: Discipline-Specific – Portfolio Management (Establishing and Leading)

Level	Description
Project Assistant	• Understands the basics of portfolio management
Project Analyst	• Understands the business needs of establishing portfolio management
Jr. Project Manager	• Articulates the costs and benefits of portfolio management
Project Manager	• Contributes to portfolio management processes • Analyzes portfolios for a variety of business purposes to come up with business insights
Senior Project / Program Manager	• Improves portfolio management processes • Designs reports and outputs to improve portfolio management
Program Director	• Independently operates a portfolio of projects for the department • Makes recommendations or decisions (in some limited cases), based on portfolio analysis

xvii. Discipline-Specific – Business Process Design

Table 38: Discipline-Specific – Business Process Design

Level	Description
Project Assistant	• Understands the purpose of business process design
Project Analyst	• Understands the importance of business processes within an organization • Analyzes select processes impacted by business, organizational, or technological change
Jr. Project Manager	• Identifies business processes impacted by business, organizational, and/or technological change • Works with internal client team members to understand and document these key processes • Suggests improvements to processes
Project Manager	• Identifies key processes impacted by business, organizational, and/or technological change • Collaborates with internal client team members in joint sessions to understand and document these key processes • Collaborates with internal client team members to create improved processes • Creates high-level and detailed process maps and schematics
Senior Project /	• Understands the key principles, best practices, and pitfalls of process design

Level	Description
Program Manager	• Understands the tradeoffs between various designs • Articulates process challenges, benefits, and consequences to the project team • Designs and re-designs processes to optimize desired consequences • Reviews and refines the work of others
Program Director	• Works with internal executives to change processes • Identifies key process design implications and consequences • Synthesizes process efforts from various areas and creates a coherent view • Develops and refines firm's methodology on process design

xviii. Discipline-Specific – Business Analysis

Table 39: Discipline-Specific – Business Analysis

Level	Description
Project Assistant	• Understands the importance of business analysis and how it fits into the overall project lifecycle
Project Analyst	• Analyzes project scope and the associated business environment to determine requirements • Documents the validated business requirements

Level	Description
Jr. Project Manager	• Works with project manager to develop detailed work breakdown structures or other techniques in order to identify the specific tasks required for implementation • Develops traceability tools and techniques to ensure alignment with implementation
Project Manager	Even though Business Analysts and Project Managers work closely on projects, their disciplines are different. Thus, in this book, I am only providing the basic business analysis skills up to Junior Project Manager.
Senior Project / Program Manager	
Program Director	

xix. Discipline-Specific – Execution Planning & Management

Table 40: Discipline-Specific – Execution Planning & Management

Level	Description
Project Assistant	• Clearly understands how to contribute to successful execution
Project Analyst	• Identifies, resolves, and/or escalates issues • Identifies key client requirements and project milestones

Level	Description
	• Articulates requirements and specifications to team members
Jr. Project Manager	• Communicates execution plans to project team members • Develops action and implementation plans for small-moderate projects with minimal supervision • Understands and accounts for requirements and specifications for small-moderate projects with minimal supervision
Project Manager	• Clearly communicates execution plans to track leads and project sponsors • Develops action and implementation plans for moderate-large projects with minimal supervision • Understands and accounts for requirements and specifications for complex projects with minimal supervision
Senior Project / Program Manager	• Leads project team members and managers in execution planning • Suggests improvements to program/project methodology • Supervises the development of action and implementation plans, requirements, and specifications • Creates detailed project resource plans that take into account people and cost • Identifies high-risk areas and suggests ways to mitigate risk

Level	Description
Program Director	• Leads project executives in execution planning and management • Advances approach to execution planning and management

xx. Discipline-Specific – Managing Implementation Vendors

Table 41: Discipline-Specific – Managing Implementation Vendors

Level	Description
Project Assistant	• Develops positive working relationship with vendors • Assists project team with vendor communication, deliverable production, and coordination
Project Analyst	• Manages select processes with vendors such as contract negotiation • Assesses vendor capabilities and performs due diligence • Facilitates communication between clients and vendors
Jr. Project Manager	• Manages vendors with partial supervision • Effectively assesses a vendor's technical capabilities • Develops expertise on at least one category of implementation vendor, such as design firms, CMS professional services,

Level	Description
	project management tools, collaboration tools, etc. • Possesses a working knowledge of implementation vendor landscape
Project Manager	• Manages vendors independently • Effectively evaluates a vendor's full capabilities, both technical and non-technical, as well as financial and strategic viability
Senior Project / Program Manager	• Negotiates service levels, contracts, scope, and price on behalf of internal clients with minimal supervision • Independently negotiates selective contracts with vendors on behalf of the client department
Program Director	• Fully manages vendor business and technical relationships • Independently negotiates large and complex contracts with vendors on behalf of the client department

xxi. Discipline-Specific – Product Management

Table 42: Discipline-Specific – Product Management

Level	Description
Project Assistant	• Clearly understands what product management consists of
Project Analyst	• Identifies product management needs
Jr. Project Manager	• Articulates the business needs of product management • Possesses a basic understanding of the key "products" required by customers
Project Manager	• Possesses a basic understanding of product management principles, processes, and lifecycles • Possesses a strong understanding of relevant products and services required by customers and how they will add value to the organization • Assesses impact of new products and product development processes to other areas of the firm
Senior Project / Program Manager	• Fully understands product management processes, tools, and templates • Leads project teams in workshops to select and prioritize features and functions of products • Identifies and mitigates potential risks for products
Program Director	• Leads full-cycle product management engagements

Level	Description
	• Communicates to senior level product managers and executives

xxii. Organizational Skills – Human Development

Table 43: Organizational Skills – Human Development

Level	Description
Project Assistant	• Actively seeks ways to develop oneself • Knows when to seek mentorship
Project Analyst	• Desires to help others within the organization • Identifies training needs, both for oneself and others within the company • Takes the initiative to work with supervisors to discuss one's developmental needs
Jr. Project Manager	• Coaches Project Assistants and Analysts • Delivers select project training • Properly confronts direct reports when needed
Project Manager	• Coaches Project Assistants, Analysts, and Junior Project Manager • Designs, develops, and delivers training
Senior Project / Program Manager	• Identifies key developmental needs of direct reports • Mentors others

Level	Description
Program Director	• Leads human development initiatives • Develops career development plans for staff

xxiii. Organizational Skills – Methodology Development

Table 44: Organizational Skills – Methodology Development

Level	Description
Project Assistant	• Appreciates and comprehends the basic needs for project management methodologies
Project Analyst	• Analyzes and evaluates value and shortcomings of methodologies • Recommends incremental changes to improve the methodologies and the underlying processes
Jr. Project Manager	• Consistently applies the methodologies to projects • Customizes methodologies as required for various project considerations and with proper approval
Project Manager	• Expertly applies methodologies to projects
Senior Project / Program Manager	• Suggests new processes or methods to improve the overall methodology

Level	Description
Program Director	• Enhances or create new methodologies as required to meet the challenges of business changes

xxiv. Organizational Skills – Cultural Change

Table 45: Organizational Skills – Cultural Change

Level	Description
Project Assistant	• Understands the core elements of firm culture, including what works and what needs to be changed
Project Analyst	• Encourages others to understand the positive and/or negative effects of change
Jr. Project Manager	• Understands the basic tools and techniques necessary for change to be more easily made • Works with others to make change happen, as directed by supervisors
Project Manager	• Possesses hands-on knowledge of the basic tools and techniques necessary for change to be more easily made • Works with supervisors to partially manage change initiatives
Senior Project / Program Manager	• Identifies gaps and issues within a firm's culture • Leads change initiatives

Level	Description
Program Director	• Develops change programs to enhance execution capability

xxv. Organizational Skills – Knowledge Management

Table 46: Organizational Skills – Knowledge Management

Level	Description
Project Assistant	• Possesses a general understanding of Continuous Improvement as well as other project management processes and tools
Project Analyst	• Possesses a working knowledge of Continuous Improvement and other project/program management processes and tools • Actively contributes to company collaboration system and uploads relevant materials in a timely fashion without being asked
Jr. Project Manager	• Identifies opportunities for knowledge capture and re-use • Maintains knowledge assets by encouraging oneself and others to actively contribute
Project Manager	• Volunteers to work on opportunities for knowledge capture and re-use

Level	Description
	• Proactively enhances knowledge assets by leading discussion forums and encouraging others to contribute to knowledge tools
Senior Project / Program Manager	• Leads knowledge management initiatives such as rethinking the structure and use of collaboration tools and designing enhanced methods of knowledge sharing • Ensures that all key knowledge is captured in the designated tools
Program Director	• Leads the development of methods, tools, and systems to enhance knowledge base

D. What are the core skill and qualification guidelines?

To function effectively in project management, one must possess certain qualifications and core skills. In this section, I will present my views on qualifications and skills required at each level of project management, as well as my suggestions for career development and PMI credentials.

I have applied this structure and guideline to multiple organizations ranging from small business firms to global consulting companies.

i. Project Assistant

Table 47: Qualification and Skill Guidelines for Project Assistant

1. Project Assistant	
Basic Qualifications	• 0 years of work experience • Degree or certificate in a technical or business field • Strong desire to learn project management
Core Skills	• Some scheduling and resource coordination experience • Strong communication skills • Strong technical writing ability • Strong research capability • Knowledge of MS Office and Basic MS Project • Strong interest in project management
Career Development Suggestions	• Your training should focus on core management and project management skills such as communication, writing, teamwork, organization, project management, etc. • Gain experience with increasingly advanced project management tasks such as scheduling, facilitating issue resolution, managing change request processes, etc.

PMI Certification Suggestions	Consider Certified Associate in Project Management (CAPM).

ii. Project Analyst

Table 48: Qualification and Skill Guidelines for Project Analyst

2. Project Analyst	
Basic Qualifications	• 2-5 years of work experience with at least 2 years in project management • Bachelor's degree in a technical field, preferably project management • Strong desire to be a project manager

Core Skills	• In addition to those listed for Project Assistant:
	  ○ Clear decision-making ability
	  ○ Strong interpersonal skills
	  ○ Good presentation skills
	  ○ Basic project management skills
	  ○ Basic knowledge of project management tools

Career Development Suggestions	• Your training should lead to the completion of the Certified Associate in Project Management (CAPM), which should focus on core project management skills

	• Complete an estimated 24-40 hours of training per year
PMI Certification Suggestions	• Strongly consider Certified Associate in Project Management (CAPM) • Depending on interests and your firm, you may also wish to consider PMI Scheduling Professional (PMI-SP), PMI Risk Management Professional (PMI-RMP), and PMI Agile Certified Practitioner (PMI-ACP) • As an alternative, you may wish to consider the business analysis discipline and start preparing for the PMI-PBA

iii. Junior Project Manager

Table 49: Qualification and Skill Guidelines for Junior Project Manager

3. Junior Project Manager	
Basic Qualifications	• 4-8 years of work experience with at least 4 years in project management • Bachelor's degree in a technical field, preferably project management • Certified Associate in Project Management (CAPM) preferably (this can be offset by 2 additional years of experience) • Strong desire to advance in the project management field

Core Skills	• In addition to those listed for Project Analyst:
	  ○ Logical decision-making
	  ○ Strong analytical thinking
	  ○ Strong presentation skills
	  ○ Strong initiative and drive
	  ○ Ability to review key project deliverables for completion and thoroughness
	  ○ Fundamental knowledge of project management and its associated skills
	  ○ Advanced knowledge of project management tools

Career Development Suggestions	• Your training should lead to the completion of the Project Management

	Professional (PMP), with a focus on core and advanced project management skills • Complete one college-level course or estimated 24-40 hours of professional training per year
PMI Certification Suggestions	• Consider skipping CAPM if you are near or have met the required years of experienced required for PMP • Consider Project Management Professional (PMP) • Depending on your interests and your firm, you may also wish to consider PMI Scheduling Professional (PMI-SP), PMI Risk Management Professional (PMI-RMP), and PMI Agile Certified Practitioner (PMI-ACP) • As an alternative, you may wish to seriously consider the business analysis discipline and start preparing for the PMI-PBA

iv. Project Manager

Table 50: Qualification and Skill Guidelines for Project Manager

4. Project Manager	
Basic Qualifications	<ul><li>8-12 years of work experience with at least 6 years in project management</li><li>Bachelor's degree in a technical field, preferably project management</li><li>Masters or advanced degree in a technical field</li><li>PMP certified preferably (this can be offset by 4 additional years of experience)</li><li>Strong desire to build a career in project management</li></ul>
Core Skills	<ul><li>In addition to those listed for Junior Project Manager:<ul><li>Strong creative thinking</li><li>Strong written communication</li><li>Ability to think strategically</li><li>Basic understanding of program management</li><li>Fundamental understanding of different project and development methodologies</li><li>Developing well-supported perspectives on project management</li></ul></li></ul>
Career Development Suggestions	<ul><li>For non-PMPs, your training should lead to the completion of the Project Management Professional (PMP)</li></ul>

	• If you are already PMP certified, focus on additional core and advanced project management skills • Complete one graduate level course or estimated 24-40 hours of professional training per year
PMI Certification Suggestions	• Project Management Professional (PMP) is highly desirable at this level • If you already have PMP, you should consider one of the specialty project management certifications such as PMI Scheduling Professional (PMI-SP), PMI Risk Management Professional (PMI-RMP), and/or PMI Agile Certified Practitioner (PMI-ACP)

v. Senior Project Manager

Table 51: Qualification and Skill Guidelines for Senior Project Manager

5. Senior Project Manager	
Basic Qualifications	• 12-14 years of work experience with at least 8 years in project management • Bachelor's degree in a technical field, preferably project management • Masters or advanced degree in a technical field preferably • Project Management Professional (PMP) preferably (this can be offset by 4 additional years of experience) • Strong desire to be a leader in the project management field

Core Skills	• In addition to those listed for Project Manager:
	  ○ Strong hands-on knowledge of program management
	  ○ Strategic planning and management skills
	  ○ Ability to assistant in methodological development
	  ○ Advanced knowledge of project management tools

Career Development Suggestions	• Your training should continue to focus on becoming an expert project manager and/or program manager

	• Complete two graduate level courses or an estimated 32-56 hours of professional training per year
PMI Certification Suggestions	• Project Management Professional (PMP) at this level is becoming essential; though you may not necessarily need it in the present job, a PMP will increase you marketability if your situation should change • You should also consider one of the specialty project management certifications such as PMI Scheduling Professional (PMI-SP), PMI Risk Management Professional (PMI-RMP), and/or PMI Agile Certified Practitioner (PMI-ACP) • If you are seeking increased responsibilities, start considering the Program Management Professional (PgMP) certification

vi. Program Director

Table 52: Qualification and Skill Guidelines for Program Director

6. Program Director	
Basic Qualifications	<ul><li>15+ years of work experience with at least 10 years in project management</li><li>Masters and bachelor degrees in business or technical field, preferably with formal training in project management</li><li>Project Management Professional (PMP). Can be offset by 4 additional years of experience OR Program Management Professional (PgMP)</li><li>Strong desire to be a leader in the program management field</li></ul>
Core Skills	<ul><li>In addition to those listed for Senior Project Manager:<ul><li>Executive communication skills</li><li>Advanced presentation skills</li><li>Advanced knowledge of project management and its associated skills</li><li>Ability to lead methodological development</li><li>Thought leadership</li><li>Facilitation skills</li><li>Strong knowledge of best practices</li></ul></li></ul>
Career Development Suggestions	<ul><li>Your training should continue to focus on becoming a leader in program/project management</li></ul>

	• Complete two college-level courses or estimated 32-56 hours of advanced professional training per year
PMI Certification Suggestions	• Program Management Professional (PgMP) is highly desirable at this level • If you are seeking growth opportunities, especially making or influencing decisions with regards to project investment, then start considering Portfolio Management Professional (PfMP)

vii. Portfolio Manager / Director

Table 53: Qualification and Skill Guidelines for Portfolio Manager / Director

7. Portfolio Manager / Director	
Basic Qualifications	• 20+ years of work experience with at least 15 years in project and program management • Masters and bachelor degrees in business or technical field, preferably with formal training in project management • Portfolio Management (PfMP) Certification is required

Core Skills	• In addition to those listed above:
	  o Strategic planning
	  o Execution planning

	○ Organizational acumen to create sustainable organizations
Career Development Suggestions	• Your training should continue to focus on becoming a leader in portfolio/program/project management • Complete two college level courses or an estimated 32-56 hours of advanced professional training per year
PMI Certification Suggestions	• Portfolio Management Professional (PfMP) is highly desirable at this level • To progress beyond portfolio management, you should look to establish a more robust project management office (PMO), improve an existing PMO, or urge your organization to create a "Chief Project Officer" role

The goal of this chapter was to provide a broad overview of the required knowledge and skill sets for project professionals. Naturally, each person and every situation is unique. My hope is that you will let this chapter serve as a roadmap as you navigate through your career in project management.

In the next chapter, I will switch gears and address some of the most common challenges in project management in an unconventional way - through storytelling.

"Tell me and I forget. Teach me and I remember. Involve me and I learn."

Benjamin Franklin

Storytelling is a powerful tool. Long before written language, our ancestors passed knowledge from one generation to the next orally through songs and stories. I have long been intrigued by the mythical power of storytelling, and since an early age have learned some of life's most importance lessons from stories.

As a practicing project, program, and portfolio manager as well as a college professor, I have experienced, witnessed, and fielded countless questions. Over the years, a pattern has emerged. I have chosen to craft four narratives – war stories, if you will – as mentioned at the beginning of the book to serve as the fictional framework through which I'd weave in these very real questions.

Throughout this book, I've argued that project management is as much an art as it is a science. Though I am by no means a fictional reader, it's time to put my money where my mouth is and try my hand at penning stories. I hope you find them both enjoyable and instructive – and if not, I'll take no offense.

Before you read each of these short stories, it may be worthwhile to review the situational context surrounding these four characters in Section IV.

Story 1: How did Terrance Lee begin his career path in project management?

On the night before his first project management class, Terrance is chatting with his friends over dinner about their upcoming project management course. His buddies seem surprised by the syllabus, which promises a heavy load of work - multiple presentations and case projects on top of quizzes, tests, and group projects. As seniors, many of them are looking forward to winding down their studies, spending more time on the job hunt, and enjoying the time until graduation. Terrance, though, is undaunted. Finishing off his slice of pizza, he explains: "Look, guys, we've learned a lot of stuff during college. We've expanded our brains and enhanced our capacity for learning. But how much of what we've learned is immediately marketable? I've applied to so many internships and jobs at this point, but nearly all of them required concrete skills and actual experience. Do you think a company is going to hire me as a manager straight out of school even though I have a management degree? Not likely."

The next day, after the project management class, Terrance hangs around to speak one-on-one with the professor. He's eager to learn how to get started in project management, knowing full well that he needs experience to make his resume more credible. Over the course of the conversation, Terrance promises his professor that he will do whatever it takes to not only perform well in the class but to gain the requisite experience through course projects and other assignments.

That night, Terrance mulls over his professor's recommendations. As he understands it, his professor's advice was fourfold:

1. Obviously, work hard and take the class seriously. One surefire way to showing commitment to the class is by taking the lead on group project assignments.
2. Consider obtaining the Certified Associate in Project Management (CAPM) credential. This certification can serve as a key differentiator in a competitive job market.
3. Look into joining a local chapter of the Project Management Institute. Regularly attend meetings to network with other professionals, and find volunteer opportunities.
4. Finally, assuming schedule permits, consider registering for an experiential learning course to be offered in the final semester of senior year. This is a great way of putting a lot of theoretical learning to work.

i. Course work

Of the professor's four recommendations, succeeding in the course work is the easiest to tackle. Terrance has always been a good student. He studies hard, carefully reads through all of the course materials, takes active part in the case study discussions, and confidently leads the group projects. To ensure his "A" for the course and to impress the professor, he even completes some extra credit.

By the end of the semester, he has amassed a working knowledge of the key project management concepts, processes, tools, and techniques. The project work gave him some hands-on experience working on project tasks such as developing work breakdown structures, analyzing resources, creating project plans, mitigating risks, and reporting on project performance.

ii. Passing the CAPM

Since the CAPM requires 23 hours of education prior to even filing an application, Terrance had to wait until the middle of the semester. Once he'd met his 23 hours, he eagerly applied for the certification. The turnaround from PMI was quick, and in five days, he received approval to take the exam. After looking at the exam availability, Terrance scheduled the exam with a Prometric testing center immediately after the final exam, knowing that this way everything would still be fresh in his mind.

But on the week before the exam, he realizes he's made a mistake. He is already exhausted from the semester's work, and while everyone else is preparing for the holidays, he still has another grueling three-hour exam. Though he toys more than once with the idea of postponing it, in the end he resolves to stick with his gut and take the test. That way, at least, he won't have to think about it over the holidays.

Terrance studies hard for the exam. Luckily, the course textbook was based on the latest Project Management Body of Knowledge (PMBOK), so much so, that the material he had learned in class closely matches that in the PMBOK. On the night before the exam, heeding his professor's advice, he heads over to the fitness center and exercises. He gets an early night's sleep and wakes up fresh. After eating a healthy and substantial breakfast of fruit, yogurt, and cereal, he drives to the training center.

Between the preparation, exercise, good sleep, and healthy breakfast, he is mentally and physically ready for the exam. Following the test-taking strategy imparted by his professor, he uses the first few minutes to perform a data dump and writes down all of the relevant information, including ITTO (Inputs, Tools, Techniques, and Outputs) of the project management knowledge areas. Then, as planned, he performs two passes through the entire exam. He does not skip any questions. Even though he has some doubts about a few answers. His manual score sheet, an exam aid suggested by his professor, shows that his likely score would be about 90% - meaning he should comfortably pass the exam.

He indeed passes, with marks of "proficient" or "moderately proficient" in all knowledge areas. Reflecting from the other side of the test, Terrance is glad he had spent the time developing an exam strategy. About two hours into the exam, he was mentally tired. All the weeks of studying for both his final exams and the CAPM had taken their toll. Since the clock keeps ticking, he didn't take any breaks and just stretched at his desk. Terrance was also grateful that he had exercised, slept well, and eaten a healthy breakfast. Not only was he mentally drained, he was also a bit hungry toward the end of the exam. Had he not eaten a substantial breakfast, he was sure his stamina would have deteriorated.

iii. Project Management Institute Local Chapters

Picking up on his hard work and commitment, Terrance's professor offered to introduce him to the local PMI chapter. But to join, Terrance had to first become a member of PMI Global. Luckily, since he's a full-time student, his membership was greatly reduced from $129 to $32. Better yet, the local chapter membership was free due to a special arrangement agreement between the local chapter and his professor. Among the many perks for the $32 membership, Terrance soon learned, was that PMI allows their members to download all the project, program, and portfolio standards, plus a few others, for free.

As a new member, Terrance finds that the local chapter offers a variety of opportunities to network, learn, and volunteer. He joined their study group to prepare for the CAPM exam. Even though the group meetings were not always consistent, he was able to meet other aspiring project managers studying for their CAPM and PMP. He attends a number of monthly chapter meetings, and particularly enjoys the professional presentations given by members and guest speakers. Terrance also volunteered on the registration team to help organize events, man the registration desk, and interact with new members.

As he develops his professional network, Terrance is learning to pick up key words with regards to employment opportunities. Though he has not yet found a job, he is learning the art of networking, and feels confident that this will lead to job prospects.

He recently heard talk of a new internal chapter project for developing a more robust outreach program. Now, with growing confidence and his CAPM firmly in hand, he thinks he may volunteer for that project as a project manager for one of the work groups. But before taking on that task, he first wants to first solidify his course schedule for the last semester of classes. The experiential learning sounds intriguing, but it may require a significant time investment. He decides to take a "wait-and-see" approach.

iv. Experiential Learning

As the professor imparted to Terrance in their first post-class conversation, one of the greatest challenges for entry-level professionals is gaining credible experience. Ideally, companies would ideally like to hire employees who can perform all the required job activities with minimal training. Training, after all, is expensive. This, the professor explained, is where the experiential learning course comes in. Through working on real projects, students are able to work independently but in a safe environment in which the professor can provide guidance and ensure quality.

As the next semester approaches, Terrance is looking forward to the experiential class. He heard that the project will be working with a local food bank and managing their annual fundraising effort. He wonders what roles will be available to him. Is the project manager position available - and would they entrust that position to a student with the CAPM certification?

Do you think Terrance is ready? Do you believe the professor made the right recommendations? Would you have followed the same recommendations, or charted a different path? Most importantly, do you believe Terrance's hard work over the course of the semester has increased his chances of landing a job post-graduation?

Story 2: How did Patricia Johnson change her career?

In the weeks following Patricia's initial thoughts of moving her career direction toward project management, she begins to conduct some online research. What she finds is overwhelming. Project management is a popular topic, and the search engine returns pages of hits from countless sources. Thinking she might begin instead with a good book, she ventures to the library, where an online search yields hundreds of choices but nothing great. She decides to call her friend who first mentioned the idea of project management to pick her brain about how to best get started. Her friend is busy working on an out-of-town project, but is still able to provide three suggestions:

1. Check out the Project Management Institute at www.pmi.org and www.projectmanagement.com
2. Investigate project opportunities at work and attempt to work on one of those projects as a team member
3. Knowing that Patricia is active in local art organizations, the friend suggests that Patricia find a project opportunity within one of these organizations

Patricia dutifully takes up her friend's suggestions. Impressed with the mission and size of PMI, she considers joining. Some of the blogs and articles on www.projectmanagment.com are excellent, though some of the challenges and risks seem scary. Still, she's undeterred. Her own quickly-growing firm has a multitude of projects. She's friendly with a project manager who she knows is working on a cross-functional project with financial implications. After speaking with her supervisor, her involvement on the team is quickly made official. Both her supervisor and the project manager are delighted to have her expertise on board with the project. As a financial expert, she'll be able to help the project determine the business requirements and act as a voice for the customer. Unfortunately, that project is still four months from launching.

Patricia was hoping to find a project within the local art organization for which she volunteers as a mentor and teacher, but to her disappointment there were no immediate projects. Then one day, in a rather unexpected place, project management crosses her path again. She's visiting her favorite art gallery in the city, whose owner is a friend-of-a-friend. As she's viewing a new exhibition by a famous local artist, she happens to overhear a conversation between the artist and the gallery owner behind a partition. Not wanting to eavesdrop, she begins to walk away, until the word "project" catches her attention.

Apparently, the artist was urging the gallery owner to curate an art exhibition at a local park in the coming season. The exhibition has been an on-and-off event, last organized two years ago. Patricia recalls attending that event herself and thinking it had been very successful. As she remembers, it had featured about 40 local artists plus another 20 artists from all over the country. Based on the conversation, Patricia gathers that the gallery owner was hesitant to take up the mantle again since the last exhibit had been a chaotic project. In the gallery owner's own words, "I had to manage the whole event myself, and I was short on schedule, resources, and funding. If you wanted me to do this again, then find me a good project assistant."

Shortly afterwards, Patricia approaches the gallery owner and inquires about the discussion, which she fesses up to overhearing. Upon Patricia's offer to assist with the project, the gallery owner warms to the idea of organizing the exhibition again. A week later, after discussions with a number of artists, the project is officially on. The gallery owner agrees to be the project manager with Patricia as his assistant. From early on, it's evident that the gallery owner is a strong project manager, and Patricia soon learns that he's actually a member of the local chapter of PMI. He develops a project charter, stakeholder analysis, communication plan, and schedule. Patricia assists him in all these project management deliverables, and in doing so, becomes quite familiar with project management concepts such as schedule, risk, issue, and even critical path.

Time passes quickly, and the day of the art exhibition arrives. Many last-minute issues arise. Due to late registrations, the number of artists exceeds the original plan and additional space has to be secured. Even worse, the weather fails to comply when it starts raining on the first day of the event. Luckily, they have a contingency plan ready and are able to move some of the exhibits indoors while placing a large tent over others. When the whole thing is said and done, the gallery owner is pleased with the event. Patricia, thrown by all the last-minute changes, is not so sure. Still, she has to admit that it is a solid accomplishment. Over 80 artists participated in the exhibition, and while there were some mumblings about this and that, nearly all of the artists believe the event was well planned and executed.

With the exhibition behind her, the project at her firm finally begins. To her team's surprise, Patricia contributes much more than her role requires. Her colleagues thought she would be a valuable asset on the financial front, but that her value wouldn't extend to other areas. Patricia proves them wrong. She drafts parts of the charter, points out some deficiencies in the stakeholder analysis, enhances the communication plan, and even finds a major scheduling error on task dependency. Most impressively, she diligently provides status updates, follows through on issue resolutions, helps other team members, and even facilitates sessions to discuss project change requests. By the time that project successfully comes to an end nearly 11 months later, the project manager openly thanks Patricia for her contributions and suggests that she should consider becoming a project manager. Her own supervisor, proud of her work, promotes Patricia to department project manager.

She doesn't have to wait very long for another project to kick in. Barely two weeks go by before her supervisor asks Patricia if she is interested in taking a leading role representing the finance area on a major customer relationship management (CRM) implementation. The project, a significant undertaking, is central to the marketing firm's ability to manage their customers. Since Patricia began at the firm three years ago, the firm had grown from five offices to eight, with an additional two overseas. More robust technological and business processes were long overdue. Though the new IT system implementation would be relatively easy, the overhaul in business processes would impact the entire firm. Patricia is told that the project will take an estimated two years to complete. The supervisor hints that if Patricia is successful in this role, she will be promoted to a more prominent one.

For the next fourteen months, Patricia works diligently on the project team and her role continues to expand. Starting as the financial team lead, she acts as the point-person for all business processes. With the encouragement of her supervisor, the project manager, and her friend who originally suggested project management for her, Patricia takes a number of courses at a local project training center. She applies for the Project Management Professional (PMP) certification as soon as she meets the requirements. She's ready.

How valuable do you believe Patricia's experience with the art exhibition was for her work on the firm's project? What were the biggest lessons learned from the art exhibition experience? Do you know of similar stories, not necessarily in project management, in which volunteer work leads to professional growth? Do you volunteer?

Story 3: How does Steve Jackson become a program manager?

Steve Jackson, a certified PMP, is rather proud of his accomplishments, having led many large projects to successful completion. But now, he is confronted with the biggest challenge of his career. The enterprise resource planning (ERP) is his largest and most complex initiative to date. It is sad to say that it is not going well. What began as an information technology project is now effectively an enterprise business reengineering initiative. Everyone in the company appears to have an opinion on the project. Most troubling to Steve is that there have been real risks to personal data, which is a hot topic. He knows that if he is to recommend change, he must do it soon. Most of the necessary changes are not due to mis-management, but the natural outcomes of the initial planning phase. But unless he raises these issues soon, they will become his problems. There is a meeting with the Steering Committee coming up in a week, and it's an opportune time to recommend changes. But what changes, and how should they be implemented?

At Isabella's (his mentor's) suggestion, Steve realizes that he needs to "think big" by reframing the organization of the project teams. Originally, he was focusing on the project deliverables, but there were too any projects each with multiple deliverables that tracking dependencies would become a full-time job. Still, these project deliverables must come together for the entire ERP to work. Following Isabella's guidance, Steve downloads and reads PMI's Standard for Program Management - 170 plus pages, which he consumes over the weekend. He also read a number of relevant articles online to familiarize himself with program management. He realizes that Isabela is correct in that the program management approach provides more relevant processes and flexibilities for managing this initiative. Steve identifies three big issues:

1. How can he ensure these individual projects are aligned with the common business objective?
2. With the multiple shifts from starting as an IT project to ending up as a business project, what are the ultimate business benefits that the company must attain?
3. How should he best govern the program?

To address the first question, Steve calls a meeting with the various team leads and junior project managers. He asks each of them three essential questions: 1) What are the individual project deliverables? 2) How do they contribute to the business objective of the program? and 3) How do these projects interact and what are the dependencies among their tasks? He facilitates a thorough review of the work breakdown structure, project plans, and the responsibility assignment matrix, often called RACI (Responsible, Accountable, Contributed, and Informed). Through this process, he discovers a number of key components that must be collectively managed by multiple project teams to ensure the proper handshake. Additionally, he discovered a number of broader concerns, such as the quality of the vendor that should be managed at the program level.

With many shifts in this initiative, the second question of ultimate business benefits would be more aptly addressed by the Steering Committee, but Steve doesn't want to ask the question unarmed with answers. Like a true professional, he wants to provide some likely albeit imperfect answers, sometimes called "strawman", so that the Steering Committee has somewhere to start.

Steve also realizes that the current Steering Committee is too heavily weighted toward the technological stakeholders. For the program to be truly successful across the business units, it requires greater representation. Perhaps most urgently, Steve recognizes that he needs help to manage an ERP of this magnitude. After making a number of fruitless inquires that resulted in very few qualified consultants, he asked Isabella for her recommendation. Isabella came through again, introducing Steve to a certified project, program and portfolio expert.

The week leading up to the meeting passes quickly, and Steve is enmeshed in preparation mode. He begins the Steering Committee meeting by outlining the changes to the project over the past period and the implications for cost, schedule, and scope. "More importantly," Steve says, "is our approach to managing this initiative. With many projects that must come together in the end, we must adopt a different mindset for organizing and managing this project." His recommendation, not surprisingly, is a program management approach that includes a restructuring of the Steering Committee itself. Plus, he openly requests additional funding to hire a consultant well-versed in program management to assist him in managing the program for the next six months.

After examining the evidence, Steve's suggestions, and the risks of failing to act, the Steering Committee agrees to give Steve the authority to hire a consultant. Steve quickly hires the consultant recommended by Isabella, and together they establish a program management framework to manage the ERP implementation.

Since he had already initiated some of the program activities through thoughtful alignment of deliverables, benefits, interdependencies, roles, and responsibilities, Steve is able to rapidly transform the management of the ERP into a program with the help of the consultant. Before leaving the program, the consultant provides Steve with many tools and best practices to guide the ERP program. He also urges Steve to consider the Program Management Professional (PgMP) credential when he meets the entrance qualifications. Steve promises to do so.

Why is a program management approach more appropriate than a project management approach for Steve's project? What would likely happen to the ERP implementation if Steve hadn't transformed the initiative to a program management framework? Was the consultant necessary? If you were Steve, what would you have done?

Story 4. Why should Isabella Garcia pursue the Portfolio Management Professional (PfMP) credential?

Isabella Garcia is a confident woman who has gradually and diligently earned her success. Though her track record is not perfect, she considers her various failures along the way to be a necessary part of growing up. She is particularly proud of three projects in her career: 1) a master data management project, which she rescued from the jaws of failure; 2) an enterprise application development project that she helped to shut down; 3) a large program with which she built a new operating unit for her company, which is now the largest and the most successful unit in the company. But now, Isabella has been promoted to head the strategic project office that effectively decides or highly influences the $100 million project investment portfolio. Even though her manager did not impart this information to her, she knows for a fact that at least two other candidates were considered for the job, and one of them is a highly certified project and program manager. But she was chosen to lead this important function because of her talent for bringing teams together and amicably resolving conflicts among warring parties. Four questions have been dominating her mind lately:

1. How can she best make sure these projects align and stay aligned with strategy?
2. What about resource management – how should she best coordinate the capability and capacity of her organization?
3. Is she ready?
4. Do other people think she is ready?

Thus far in her career, she has largely shied away from the project management certifications. She appreciates the strong project managers on her team, many of whom are certified.

She is familiar with the Project Management Institute and has even attended some meetings. Last September, in fact, she was the guest speaker at a local chapter and presented her latest work on the need for improved business execution, which was well received. At that conference, she became intrigued by a new certification called Portfolio Management Professional (PfMP). She was pleasantly surprised to learn that PMI had finally introduced a certification that is more suitable to the needs of senior project professionals. However, that was before she earned her promotion, at which time her thoughts on the certification fell by the wayside.

Now, as Isabella is getting ready to take on her new role, she regrets not pursuing the certification sooner. She is confident in her capabilities and believes she can effectively align projects with strategy and manage resources and capacity. She believes that she is ready - but do others feel the same way? She knows that some of her colleagues are questioning their manager's choice of selecting her for this role, and this greatly upsets her. At a recent company outing, she even overheard one of the other candidates boasting of his project and program management credentials. She begins to doubt herself, and wonders if obtaining the certification would allay her fears and those of others. Her qualifications make her more than suitable for the PfMP credential, as she has exceeded the required business experience and has been managing a multi-million dollar portfolio for well over eight years.

Wishing to complete the certification quickly, she begins to research training companies who offer bootcamps to help her prepare. To her surprise, she finds only a few training companies that offered PfMP training. She contacts all of them. Though one company claims to offer training, they fail to provide a definitive date or instructor. Another company had trained only a few people and was not a PMI-approved Registered Education Provider (R.E.P.). Finally, she finds a PMI Registered Education Provider that offers a dual approach, both online and in class. She quickly starts the application process, signs up for the training course, and delves into the Standard for Portfolio Management and other recommended books.

At first, she studies these books for the purpose of passing the exam. But she quickly acknowledges the wealth of knowledge contained in the Standard for Portfolio Management and other books. The structures and processes help Isabella re-organize her experiences into a more cohesive knowledge base. She finds the training course to be excellent; not only does the course discuss tasks in detail, but it also addresses the question of "why" certain activities occur. She finds he modular approach proffered by the training course to be much better suited for her schedule. She takes the instructor's recommendations seriously, including sitting for practice exams, developing her test-taking strategies, and thoroughly studying the materials. On the day of the exam, she knows she is ready.

Looking back, she still believes she was ready for the job, even without the certification. But the information she gained in the process of studying for the Portfolio Management Professional certification surely helped to consolidate her knowledge and boost her confidence. Plus, she kind of likes the shiny new certification hanging in her new office.

Even though Isabella clearly knew the importance of project management and its certifications, why did she not pursue any of them earlier? Do you think she was wrong not to do so? Did she ultimately decide to pursue PfMP for the right reasons? Should professionals pursue certifications purely for the sake of having a brand new certificate to hang on their walls?

These stories are based on real people, scenarios, and problems weaved together to highlight the important concepts from the earlier chapters. I hope through these stories, you are able to customize and apply the suggestions and recommendations throughout this book.

Project management is a challenging career. But the rewards are many. Remember, fortune favors the brave. Good luck and boldly march forward. I hope this book serves as an invaluable guide as you climb the project management career ladder.

Appendix A: List of PMI Chapters and Potential Chapters

For the most current list of PMI chapters, visit www.pmi.org/membership/chapters-pmi-chapters.aspx.

Asia Pacific

Country	Chapter Name	Charter Year	Website URL	Annual Fee
Australia	Adelaide, South Australia Chapter	2003	www.pmiadelaide.org	$50.00
Australia	Canberra, Australia Chapter	2002	http://www.pmicanberra.org	$50.00
Australia	Melbourne, Australia Chapter	1996	http://www.melbourne.pmi.org.au/	$60.00
Australia	Queensland Australia Chapter	1999	http://www.pmiqld.org	$50.00
Australia	Sydney, Australia Chapter	1997	http://www.pmisydney.org	$60.00
Australia	Western Australia Chapter	2001	http://www.wapmi.org.au	$60.00

Country	Chapter Name	Charter Year	Website URL	Annual Fee
Bangladesh	Bangladesh Chapter	2013	http://www.pmi.org.bd	$15.00
Hong Kong	Hong Kong Chapter	1998	http://pmi.org.hk/Default.aspx	$25.00
India	Bangalore India Chapter	1999	http://www.pmibangalorechapter.org	$12.00
India	Chennai Chapter	2002	http://www.pmichennai.org	$15.00
India	Mumbai Chapter	2001	http://pmimumbaichapter.org	$10.00
India	North India Chapter	2003	http://www.pminorthindia.org	$10.00
India	Pearl City, Hyderabad Chapter	2001	http://www.pmi-pcc.org	$10.00
India	Pune-Deccan India Chapter	2005	http://www.pmipunechapter.org	$10.00
India	Trivandrum, Kerala Chapter	2004	http://www.pmikerala.org	$ 5.00
India	West Bengal Chapter	2012	http://www.pmiwbc.org	$10.00
Indonesia	Indonesia Chapter	1996	http://www.pmi-indonesia.org	$15.00
Japan	Japan Chapter	1998	https://www.pmi-japan.org/	$50.00
Malaysia	Malaysia Chapter	1994	http://www.pmi.org.my	$20.00
Mongolia	Mongolia Chapter	2014	http://www.pmimongolia.mn	$36.00

Country	Chapter Name	Charter Year	Website URL	Annual Fee
New Zealand	Chapters - New Zealand	1994	http://www.pmi.org.nz	$60.00
Pakistan	Islamabad, Pakistan Chapter	2002	http://www.pmiislamabad.org	$15.00
Pakistan	Karachi Pakistan Chapter	2006	http://www.pmikarachi.org	$20.00
Pakistan	Lahore, Pakistan Chapter	2004	http://www.pmilhr.org.pk	$10.00
Philippines	Philippines Chapter	1996	http://www.pmi.org.ph	$20.00
Singapore	Singapore Chapter	2002	http://www.pmi.org.sg	$40.00
South Korea	South Korea Chapter	2012	http://www.pmikorea.kr	$33.00
Sri Lanka	Colombo, Sri Lanka Chapter	2005	http://www.pmicolombo.org	$10.00
Taiwan	Taipei, Taiwan Chapter	1999	http://www.pmi.org.tw	$35.00
Thailand	Thailand Chapter	2001	http://www.pmithai.org	$25.00
Vietnam	Vietnam Potential Chapter		http://www.pmi.org/ChapterAccess	$10.00

Europe, Middle East, and Africa

Country	Chapter Name	Charter Year	Website URL	Annual Fee
Austria	Austria Chapter	2000	http://www.pmi-austria.org	$30.00
Bahrain				
Belgium	Belgium Chapter	1998	http://www.pmi-belgium.be	$35.00
Bosnia and Herzegovina	Bosnia and Herzegovina Potential Chapter		http://www.pmi.ba	$20.00
Bulgaria	Bulgaria Chapter	2010	http://www.pmi.bg	$30.00
Cameroon	Cameroon Chapter	2014	http://www.pmi-cameroon.org	$30.00

Country	Chapter Name	Charter Year	Website URL	Annual Fee
Croatia	Zagreb Croatia Chapter	2005	http://www.pmi-croatia.hr	$15.00
Cyprus	Cyprus Potential Chapter		http://www.pmi.org/ChapterAccess	$25.00
Czech Republic	Czech Republic Chapter	2012	http://www.pmi.cz	$10.00
Denmark	Denmark Chapter	2000	http://www.pmi-dk.org	$30.00
Egypt	Egypt Potential Chapter		http://www.pmi.org/ChapterAccess	$20.00
Finland	Finland Chapter	2005	http://www.pmifinland.org	$10.00
France	France Chapter	2013	http://www.pmi-france.org	$30.00
Germany	Berlin/Brandenburg Chapter	2004	http://www.pmi-berlin.org	$25.00

Country	Chapter Name	Charter Year	Website URL	Annual Fee
Germany	Cologne Chapter	2003	http://www.pmicc.de	$20.00
Germany	Frankfurt Chapter	1988	http://www.pmifc.de	$20.00
Germany	Munich Germany Chapter	1998	http://www.pmi-muc.de	$25.00
Ghana	Ghana Chapter	2011	http://www.pmi-ghana.org	$30.00
Greece	Greece Chapter	2002	http://www.pmi-greece.org	$30.00
Hungary	Budapest, Hungarian Chapter	2003	http://www.pmi.hu	$50.00
Ireland	Ireland Chapter	1998	http://www.pmi-ireland.org	$30.00

Country	Chapter Name	Charter Year	Website URL	Annual Fee
Israel	Israel Chapter	1996	http://www.pmi.org.il	$30.00
Italy	Northern Italy Chapter	1996	http://www.pmi-nic.org	$36.00
Italy	Rome Italy Chapter	1996	http://www.pmi-rome.org	$36.00
Italy	Southern Italy Chapter	2004	http://www.pmi-sic.org	$31.00
Ivory Coast	Ivory Coast Potential Chapter		http://www.pmi.org/ChapterAccess	$30.00
Jordan	Jordan Chapter	2007	http://pmijo.org	$20.00
Kazakhstan	Kazakhstan Potential Chapter		http://pmi.master24.kz/	$ -
Kenya	Kenya Chapter	2014	http://www.pmikenya.com	$20.00

Country	Chapter Name	Charter Year	Website URL	Annual Fee
Kuwait	Arabian Gulf Chapter			
Lebanon	Lebanon Chapter	2006	http://www.pmilebanonchapter.org	$20.00
Lithuania	Lithuania Chapter	2012	http://www.pmi-lithuania.org	$20.00
Luxembourg	Luxembourg Chapter			
Morocco	Morocco Chapter	2010	http://www.pmimaroc.org	$30.00
Netherlands	Netherlands Chapter	2001	http://www.pmi-netherlands-chapter.org	$40.00
Nigeria	Nigeria Chapter	2005	http://www.pminigeria.org	$40.00
Norway	Norway Chapter	2000	http://www.pmi-no.org	$30.00

Country	Chapter Name	Charter Year	Website URL	Annual Fee
Oman				
Poland	Poland Chapter	2003	http://www.pmi.org.pl	$20.00
Portugal	Portugal Chapter	2003	http://www.pmi-portugal.org	$25.00
Qatar				
Romania	Romania Chapter	2002	http://www.pmi.ro	$30.00
Russia	Moscow, Russia Chapter	1998	http://www.pmi.ru	$ -
Russia	St. Petersburg Potential Chapter		http://www.pmi.org.ru	$ -
Saudi Arabia				

Country	Chapter Name	Charter Year	Website URL	Annual Fee
Serbia	Serbia Chapter	2003	http://www.pmi-serbia.rs/	$20.00
Slovakia	Slovakia Chapter	2012	http://www.pmi.sk	$20.00
Slovenia	Slovenia, Ljubljana Chapter	2002	http://www.pmi-slo.org	$11.00
South Africa	South Africa Chapter	1981	http://www.pmi.org.za	$30.00
Spain	Barcelona, Spain Chapter	2004	http://www.pmi-bcn.org	$37.00
Spain	Madrid, Spain Chapter	2003	http://www.pmi-mad.org	$40.00
Spain	Valencia, Spain Chapter	2005	http://www.pmi-valencia.org	$30.00
Sweden	Sweden Chapter	1998	http://www.pmi-se.org	$25.00

Country	Chapter Name	Charter Year	Website URL	Annual Fee
Switzerland	Switzerland Chapter	2001	http://www.pmi-switzerland.ch	$35.00
Tanzania	Tanzania Potential Chapter		http://www.pmi.org/ChapterAccess	$30.00
Turkey	Turkey Chapter	1997	http://www.pmi.org.tr	$25.00
Uganda	Uganda Chapter	2014	http://www.pmiuganda.org	$50.00
Ukraine	Kyiv Chapter	2004	http://pmiukraine.org/	$ -
United Kingdom	United Kingdom Chapter	1995	http://www.pmi.org.uk	$40.00

Latin America

Country	Chapter Name	Charter Year	Website URL	Annual Fee
El Salvador	El Salvador Potential Chapter	Potential	http://www.pmi-elsalvador.org	$20.00
Argentina	Buenos Aires, Argentina Chapter	1996	http://www.pmi.org.ar	$25.00
Argentina	Nuevo Cuyo Argentina Chapter	2010	http://www.pminuevocuyo.org/	$25.00
Bolivia	Santa Cruz, Bolivia Chapter	2015	http://www.pmisantacruz.org/	$25.00
Brazil	Brasil, Distrito Federal Chapter	2001	http://www.pmidf.org	$20.00
Brazil	Brazil, Bahia Chapter	2003	http://www.pmiba.org.br	$20.00
Brazil	Espirito Santo Brazil Chapter	2005	http://www.pmies.org.br	$20.00

Country	Chapter Name	Charter Year	Website URL	Annual Fee
Brazil	Fortaleza Ceara Brazil Chapter	2005	http://www.pmice.org.br	$20.00
Brazil	Goiania,Goias, Brazil Chapter	2005	http://www.pmiba.org.br	$20.00
Brazil	Joinville, Santa Catarina, Brazil Chapter	2003	http://www.pmies.org.br	$20.00
Brazil	Manaus Brazil Chapter	2003	http://www.pmice.org.br	$20.00
Brazil	Mato Grosso, Brazil Chapter	2015	http://www.pmimt.org.br	$20.00
Brazil	Minas Gerais, Brazil Chapter	1999	http://www.pmimg.org.br	$20.00
Brazil	Parana Chapter	2001	http://www.pmipr.org.br	$20.00

Country	Chapter Name	Charter Year	Website URL	Annual Fee
Brazil	Recife, Pernambuco Brazil Chapter	2003	http://www.pmipe.org.br	$20.00
Brazil	Rio de Janeiro, Brazil Chapter	1999	http://www.pmirio.org.br	$20.00
Brazil	Rio de Janeiro, Brazil Chapter	2001	http://www.pmirs.org.br	$20.00
Brazil	Sao Paulo, Brazil Chapter	1998	http://www.pmisp.org.br	$20.00
Brazil	Sergipe, Brazil Chapter	2012	http://www.pmise.org.br	$20.00
Chile	Santiago, Chile Chapter	1997	http://www.pmi.cl	$25.00
Colombia	Antioquia, Colombia Potential Chapter		http://www.pmi.org/ChapterAccess	$30.00
Colombia	Bogota, Colombia Chapter	1998	http://www.pmicolombia.org	$30.00

Country	Chapter Name	Charter Year	Website URL	Annual Fee
Costa Rica	Costa Rica Chapter	2001	http://www.pmicr.org	$20.00
Dominican Republic	Dominican Republic Chapter	2011	http://www.pmird.org.do	$25.00
Ecuador	Ecuador Chapter	2010	http://www.pmiecuador.org	$25.00
Guatemala	Guatemala Chapter	2014	http://www.pmi.org.gt	$20.00
Honduras	Honduras Potential Chapter		http://www.pmihonduras.org	$20.00
Mexico	Guadalajara Mexico Chapter	2005	http://www.pmigdl.org	$20.00
Mexico	Manuel Del Río Díaz	1997	http://www.pminl.org	$20.00
Mexico	Mexico Chapter	1996	http://www.pmichapters-mexico.org	$30.00
Mexico	Puebla, Mexico Chapter	2004	http://www.facebook.com/PMICapituloPuebla	$20.00
Mexico	Sinaloa, Mexico Chapter	2011	http://www.pmisinaloa.org	$20.00
Nicaragua	Nicaragua Potential Chapter		http://www.pminicaragua.org	$25.00

Country	Chapter Name	Charter Year	Website URL	Annual Fee
Panama	Panama Chapter	2004	http://www.pmi-panama.org	$25.00
Paraguay	Asunción, Paraguay Chapter	2011	http://www.pmi.org.py	$20.00
Peru	Cajamarca, Peru Chapter	2014	http://www.pmicajamarca.org	$15.00
Peru	Lima, Peru Chapter	1999	http://www.pmi.org.pe	$18.00
Peru	Southern Region, Peru Chapter	2014	http://www.pmisurperu.org	$15.00
Uruguay	Montevideo, Uruguay Chapter	2001	http://pmi.uy/	$20.00
Venezuela	Venezuela Chapter	1994	http://www.pmi.org.ve	$15.00

North America

Canada

Province	Chapter Name	Charter Year	Website URL	Annual Fee
British Columbia	Canadian West Coast Chapter	1979	http://www.pmi.bc.ca	$30.00
British Columbia	Vancouver Island Chapter	1996	http://www.pmivi.org	$30.00
Alberta	Northern Alberta Chapter	1981	http://pminac.com	$20.00
Alberta	Southern Alberta Chapter	1980	http://www.pmisac.com	$30.00
Manitoba	Manitoba Chapter	1994	http://pmimanitoba.org	$25.00
New Brunswick	New Brunswick Chapter	2000	http://www.pminb.ca	$25.00
Newfoundland & Labrador	Newfoundland & Labrador Chapter	2001	http://www.pminl.ca	$25.00

Province	Chapter Name	Charter Year	Website URL	Annual Fee
Nova Scotia	Nova Scotia, Canada Chapter	1998	http:\\www.pmins.ca	$30.00
Ontario	Canada's Technology Triangle Chapter	2001	http://www.pmi-ctt.org	$25.00
Ontario	Durham Highlands Chapter	2002	http://pmi-dhc.ca	$20.00
Ontario	Lakeshore, Ontario Chapter	1999	http://www.pmi-lakeshore.org	$25.00
Ontario	Ottawa Valley Chapter	1985	http://www.pmiovoc.org	$25.00
Ontario	South Western Ontario Chapter	1998	http://www.pmiswoc.org	$30.00
Ontario	Southern Ontario Chapter	1975	http://www.soc.pmi.on.ca	$30.00
Quebec	Levis, Quebec Chapter	1995	https://pmiquebec.qc.ca/	$30.00
Quebec	Montreal Chapter	1977	http://www.pmimontreal.org	$30.00
Saskatchewan	North Saskatchewan Chapter	2000	http://pminorthsask.com	$20.00
Saskatchewan	Regina/S.Saskatchewan Chapter	1996	http://www.pmisouthsask.org	$30.00

United States

State	Chapter Name	Charter Year	Website URL	Annual Fee
Alabama	Central Alabama Chapter	1995	http://pmicac.org	$25.00
Alabama	Emerald Coast, FL Chapter	2009	http://www.pmiemeraldcoastfl.org	$25.00
Alabama	North Alabama Chapter	1990	http://www.pmi-nac.org/homepage	$20.00
Alabama	South Alabama Chapter	2004	http://www.pmimontgomery.org	$25.00
Alaska	Alaska Chapter	1986	http://www.pmiak.org	$30.00
Arizona	Phoenix Chapter	1978	http://www.phx-pmi.org	$30.00
Arizona	Tucson, Arizona Chapter	1997	http://PMI-Tucson.org	$20.00
Arkansas	Central Arkansas Chapter	1998	http://www.pmiarkansas.org	$25.00
Arkansas	Northwest Arkansas Chapter	2005	http://www.nwapmi.org/	$25.00

State	Chapter Name	Charter Year	Website URL	Annual Fee
California	California Central Coast Chapter	2000	http://www.pmi-4c.org	$30.00
California	California Central Valley Chapter	2010	http://www.pmi-ccvc.org	$30.00
California	California Inland Empire Chapter	2002	http://pmicie.org	$30.00
California	Los Angeles Chapter	1974	http://www.pmi-la.org	$30.00
California	Monterey Bay Chapter	2004	http://www.pmi-mbay.org	$30.00
California	Orange County Chapter	1989	http://www.pmi-oc.org	$35.00
California	Sacramento Valley Chapter	1989	http://www.pmi-svc.org	$30.00
California	San Diego Chapter	1986	http://www.pmi-sd.org/	$35.00
California	San Francisco Bay Area Chapter	1974	http://www.pmi-sfbac.org/	$30.00

State	Chapter Name	Charter Year	Website URL	Annual Fee
California	Silicon Valley, CA Chapter	1997	http://www.pmisv.org/	$35.00
California	Wine Country Chapter	2000	http://www.pmi-wcc.org	$30.00
Colorado	Mile-Hi Chapter	1978	http://www.pmimilehi.org	$25.00
Colorado	Pike's Peak Regional, Colorado Chapter	1997	http://www.pmipprc.org	$25.00
Connecticut	Southern New England Chapter	1983	http://www.snec-pmi.org	$25.00
Delaware	Delaware Valley Chapter	1979	http://www.pmi-dvc.org	$25.00
Florida	Central Florida Chapter	1994	http://www.pmicfc.org	$30.00
Florida	Emerald Coast, FL Chapter	2009	http://www.pmiemeraldcoastfl.org	$25.00
Florida	Florida Suncoast Chapter	1997	http://www.suncoastpmi.org	$30.00

State	Chapter Name	Charter Year	Website URL	Annual Fee
Florida	Northeast Florida Chapter	1995	http://www.pmi-nefl.org	$35.00
Florida	South Florida Chapter	1986	http://www.southfloridapmi.org	$25.00
Florida	Space Coast, Florida Chapter	2002	http://www.pmispacecoast.org	$25.00
Florida	Tallahassee, Florida Chapter	2003	http://www.pmitlh.org	$25.00
Florida	Tampa Bay, Florida Chapter	1992	http://www.pmi-tampabay.org	$25.00
Georgia	Atlanta Chapter	1981	http://www.pmiatlanta.org	$30.00
Georgia	Augusta Aiken Chapter	1991	http://www.pmiaugustaaiken.org/	$20.00
Georgia	Columbus, Georgia Chapter	1996	http://www.pmicolumbusga.org	$25.00
Georgia	Savannah, GA Chapter	1999	http://www.pmisavannah.org	$20.00

State	Chapter Name	Charter Year	Website URL	Annual Fee
Hawaii	Honolulu, Hawaii Chapter	1998	http://www.pmihnl.org	$20.00
Idaho	Eastern Idaho Chapter	1987	http://socaljohhny@gmail.com	$20.00
Idaho	Western Idaho Chapter	1998	http://pmiwic.org	$20.00
Illinois	Central Illinois Chapter	1998	http://www.pmi-cic.org	$20.00
Illinois	Chicagoland Chapter	1977	http://www.pmi-chicagoland.org	$35.00
Indiana	Calumet Chapter	2003	http://www.pmi-calumet.org	$30.00
Indiana	Central Indiana Chapter	1988	http://www.pmicic.org	$25.00
Indiana	Michiana Chapter	2004	http://www.pmimichiana.org	$25.00
Indiana	Northeast Indiana Chapter	1997	http://www.pmi-neic.org	$20.00
Indiana	Southwestern Indiana Chapter	1998	http://president@pmiswic.org	$25.00

State	Chapter Name	Charter Year	Website URL	Annual Fee
Iowa	Central Iowa Chapter	1992	http://www.pmi-centraliowa.org	$30.00
Iowa	Eastern Iowa Chapter	1996	http://pmieasterniowa.org/	$30.00
Iowa	Quad City Area Chapter	2001	http://www.pmiqcareachapter.org	$50.00
Kansas	KC Mid America Chapter	1993	http://kcpmichapter.org/index.php?bypassCookie=1	$25.00
Kansas	Wichita, Kansas Chapter	1998	http://www.pmiwichita.org	$20.00
Kentucky	Kentuckiana Chapter	1997	http://www.kipmi.org	$30.00
Kentucky	Kentucky Bluegrass Chapter	1998	http://www.pmibluegrass.org	$25.00
Louisiana	Baton Rouge, LA Chapter	1997	http://www.pmibatonrouge.org	$30.00
Louisiana	Greater New Orleans Chapter	1990	http://www.pmigno.org	$30.00

State	Chapter Name	Charter Year	Website URL	Annual Fee
Louisiana	Northern Louisiana Chapter	2015	http://pminorthernla.org/	$25.00
Maine	Maine Chapter	1985	http://pmimaine.org	$25.00
Maryland	Baltimore, MD Chapter	1995	http://pmibaltimore.org	$20.00
Maryland	Delaware Valley Chapter	1979	http://www.pmi-dvc.org	$25.00
Maryland	Montgomery County, MD Chapter	2003	http://www.pmimontgomerycountymd.org	$20.00
Maryland	Silver Spring Chapter	2001	https://www.pmissc.org/	$20.00
Maryland	Southern Maryland Chapter	2000	http://www.pmisomd.org/	$20.00
Maryland	Washington, DC Chapter	1978	http://www.pmiwdc.org	$35.00
Massachusetts	Central Mass Chapter	2003	http://www.pmicmass.org	$25.00

State	Chapter Name	Charter Year	Website URL	Annual Fee
Massachusetts	Mass Bay Chapter	1978	http://www.PMIMassBay.org	$25.00
Michigan	Great Lakes Chapter	1979	http://www.pmiglc.org	$20.00
Michigan	Michigan Capital Area Chapter	1999	http://www.pmi-mcac.org	$20.00
Michigan	Michigan Huron Valley Chapter	2002	http://www.pmi-hvc.org	$20.00
Michigan	Michigan Thumb Chapter	1996	http://www.pmi-thumbchapter.org	$20.00
Michigan	Western Michigan Chapter	1993	http://www.wmpmi.org	$25.00
Minnesota	Minnesota Chapter	1984	http://www.pmi-mn.org	$30.00
Mississippi	Central Mississippi Chapter	2012	http://www.pmicms.org	$30.00

State	Chapter Name	Charter Year	Website URL	Annual Fee
Mississippi	Mississippi Gulf Coast Potential Chapter	2015	http://www.pmimgc.org	$25.00
Missouri	KC Mid America Chapter	1993	ttp://kcpmichapter.org/index.php?bypassCookie=1	$25.00
Missouri	Metropolitan St. Louis Chapter	1994	http://www.stlpmi.org	$30.00
Missouri	Mid-Missouri Chapter	2000	http://www.pmimidmo.org	$20.00
Missouri	Southwest Missouri Chapter	2010	http://www.pmiswmo.org	$20.00
Montana	Montana Chapter	2009	http://pmimtchapter.org	$35.00
Nebraska	Heartland (NE) Chapter	1993	http://www.pmiheartland.org	$30.00
Nebraska	Mid-Nebraska Chapter	2001	http://www.pmimidnebraska.org/	$20.00
Nevada	Northern Nevada Chapter	2009	http://www.pmi-nnv.org	$30.00

State	Chapter Name	Charter Year	Website URL	Annual Fee
Nevada	Southern Nevada Chapter	1994	http://www.pmi-snc.org	$40.00
New Hampshire	New Hampshire Chapter	2001	http://www.pmi-nh.org	$25.00
New Jersey	New Jersey Chapter	1982	http://www.pminj.org	$20.00
New Mexico	Otowi Bridge, NM Chapter	1995	http://pmi-ob.org/	$20.00
New Mexico	Rio Grande Chapter	1985	http://www.pmirgc.org	$20.00
New York	Binghamton, NY Chapter	1998	http://www.pmi-binghamton.org/	$30.00
New York	Buffalo, NY Chapter	1998	http://www.pmibuffalo.org	$30.00
New York	Hudson Valley, NY Chapter	1996	http://pmihvc.org	$25.00
New York	Long Island, NY Chapter	2000	http://www.pmilic.org	$35.00
New York	New York City Chapter	1986	http://Www.pminyc.org	$35.00

State	Chapter Name	Charter Year	Website URL	Annual Fee
New York	Rochester Chapter	1985	http://www.pmirochester.org	$35.00
New York	Syracuse Chapter	1986	http://www.pmi-syracuse.org	$25.00
New York	Upstate New York Chapter	1977	http://www.pmiuny.org	$30.00
New York	Westchester, NY Chapter	2003	http://www.pmiwestchester.org	$25.00
North Carolina	Metrolina Chapter	1985	http://pmi-metrolina.com/index.php	$25.00
North Carolina	NC Piedmont Triad Chapter	1990	http://www.pmitriadnc.org	$25.00
North Carolina	North Carolina Chapter	1985	http://www.ncpmi.org	$25.00
Ohio	Central Ohio Chapter	1975	http://www.pmicoc.org	$25.00

State	Chapter Name	Charter Year	Website URL	Annual Fee
Ohio	Dayton/Miami Valley, Ohio Chapter	1998	http://www.daytonpmi.org	$25.00
Ohio	Northeast Ohio Chapter	1990	http://www.pmineo.org/	$25.00
Ohio	Southwest Ohio Chapter	1989	http://pmiswohio.org/	$20.00
Ohio	Western Lake Erie Chapter	2001	http://www.pmiwlec.org	$25.00

State	Chapter Name	Charter Year	Website URL	Annual Fee
Oklahoma	Oklahoma City Chapter	2000	http://www.pmiokc.org	$25.00
Oklahoma	Tulsa Chapter	1990	http://www.pmitulsa.org	$25.00
Oregon	Portland Chapter	1983	http://www.pmi-portland.org	$25.00
Oregon	Willamette Valley, OR Chapter	1997	http://www.pmiwv.org/	$20.00
Pennsylvania	Delaware Valley Chapter	1979	http://www.pmi-dvc.org	$25.00
Pennsylvania	Erie, PA Chapter	2003	http://pmierie.org	$25.00
Pennsylvania	Keystone, PA Chapter	1995	http://www.pmi-keystone.org	$25.00
Pennsylvania	Pittsburgh Chapter	1980	http://www.pittsburghpmi.org	$35.00
Puerto Rico	San Juan, Puerto Rico Chapter	1998	http://www.pmipr.org	$40.00

State	Chapter Name	Charter Year	Website URL	Annual Fee
Rhode Island	Ocean State Chapter	1999	http://www.oceanstatepmi.org/	$25.00
South Carolina	Charleston, SC Chapter	2000	http://pmi-charleston.org	$25.00
South Carolina	Palmetto Chapter	1985	http://www.pmipalmetto.org/	$30.00
South Carolina	South Carolina Midlands Chapter	1996	http://www.pmi-midlands.org/	$20.00
South Dakota	Sioux Empire, South Dakota Chapter	2004	http://www.pmisd.org	$25.00
Tennessee	Chattanooga Chapter	2003	http://www.chattanoogapmi.org	$25.00
Tennessee	East Tennessee Chapter	1986	http://www.etpmi.org	$20.00
Tennessee	Memphis, TN Chapter	1999	http://www.pmimemphis.org	$25.00

State	Chapter Name	Charter Year	Website URL	Annual Fee
Tennessee	Nashville, TN Chapter	1996	http://www.pminashville.org/	$25.00
Texas	Alamo Chapter	1995	http://www.alamopmi.org	$25.00
Texas	Amarillo, Texas Chapter	1997	http://pmiamarillo.org	$35.00
Texas	Austin Chapter	1992	http://www.pmiaustin.org	$25.00
Texas	Clearlake/Galveston Chapter	2001	http://pmiclg.org/index.php	$25.00
Texas	Coastal Bend Chapter	2001	http://pmicoastalbend.org	$25.00
Texas	Dallas Chapter	1984	http://www.pmidallas.org	$20.00
Texas	Fort Worth Chapter	1992	http://www.fwpmi.org	$25.00
Texas	Houston Chapter	1974	http://www.pmihouston.org	$37.00
Texas	Sun City, TX Chapter	2015	http://www.pmielpaso.org	$25.00
Texas	West Texas Chapter	2010	http://www.pmiwtx.org	$25.00

State	Chapter Name	Charter Year	Website URL	Annual Fee
Utah	Northern Utah Chapter	1997	http://www.projectmanager.org	$20.00
Vermont	Champlain Valley, VT Chapter	1997	http://pmicv.org	$20.00
Virginia	Central Virginia Chapter	1996	http://www.pmicvc.org	$30.00
Virginia	Hampton Roads Chapter	1998	http:\\www.pmihr.org	$30.00
Virginia	Southwest Virginia Chapter	2003	http://www.pmi-swva.org	$30.00
Virginia	Washington, DC Chapter	1978	http://www.pmiwdc.org	$35.00
Washington	Columbia River Basin Chapter	1994	http://www.crb-pmi.org	$25.00
Washington	Inland Northwest Chapter	2001	http://www.pmiinw.org	$25.00
Washington	Mt. Baker, WA Chapter	2003	http://www.mountbaker-pmi.org	$25.00

State	Chapter Name	Charter Year	Website URL	Annual Fee
Washington	Olympia, Washington Chapter	2005	http://www.pmiolympia.org	$30.00
Washington	Puget Sound Chapter	1984	http://www.pspmi.org	$30.00
Washington, D.C.	Washington, DC Chapter	1978	http://www.pmiwdc.org	$35.00
West Virginia	West Virginia/Ohio Valley Chapter	1996	http://wvovpmi.org	$20.00
Wisconsin	La Crosse - Rochester Chapter	2003	http://www.pmilacrosse-rochester.org/	$25.00
Wisconsin	Madison/S. Central WI Chapter	1991	http://www.pmi-madison.org/	$25.00
Wisconsin	Milwaukee/SE WI Chapter	2000	http://www.pmi-milwaukee.org	$25.00
Wisconsin	Northeast Wisconsin Chapter	2002	http://www.pmi-new.org/	$25.00

Other Chapters in North America

Country	Chapter Name	Charter Year	Website URL	Annual Fee
Jamaica	Jamaica Chapter	1999	http://www.pmijamaica.org	$35.00
Trinidad	Southern Caribbean Chapter	1999	http://www.pmiscc.org	$20.00

Appendix B: List of Useful References

This section summarizes the important sources of information mentioned throughout the book.

#	Description	URL
1	Project Management Institute	www.pmi.org
	- About certifications	www.pmi.org/certification.aspx
	- About PMI membership	www.pmi.org/membership.aspx
	- About PMBOK® Guide and its Standards	www.pmi.org/PMBOK-Guide-and-Standards.aspx
	- Continuing Certification Requirements (CCR) Handbook	www.pmi.org/~/media/PDF/Certifications/handbooks/ccr-certification-requirements-handbook.ashx
2	AXELOS	www.axelos.com/
	- PRINCE2 (Project Management)	www.axelos.com/best-practice-solutions/prince2
	- PRINCE2 Agile (Agile Project Management)	www.axelos.com/best-practice-

#	Description	URL
		solutions/prince2/prince2-agile
	- MSP (Program Management)	www.axelos.com/best-practice-solutions/msp
	- MoP (Portfolio Management)	www.axelos.com/best-practice-solutions/mop
3	PMO Advisory LLC	www.pmoadvisory.com
	- Free resources	www.pmoadvisory.com/free-resources
	- Training (PMP, PfMP, PgMP, PMI-RMP, etc.)	www.pmoadvisory.com/training
	- Blog and latest ideas	www.pmoadvisory.com/blog
	- Self Diagnostic	www.pmoadvisory.com/training/readiness

Index

References

[1] McGrath, R., (2013). The Pace of Technology Adoption is Speeding Up, November 25, 2013, Harvard Business Review, https://hbr.org/2013/11/the-pace-of-technology-adoption-is-speeding-up/.

[2] PMI Salary Survey 2015. https://www.pmi.org/~/media/PDF/learning/project-management-salary-survey-2015.ashx

[3] ESI Annual Salary Survey, 2013, http://www.esi-intl.com/~/media/files/public-site/us/research-reports/esi-2013-project-manager-salary-and-development-survey.

[4] To determine the 2015 salary, I used average starting salary increase from National Association of College and Employers (NACE). According to NACE, the average increase was 1.2% from 2013-2014. See https://www.naceweb.org/s04022014/starting-salary-class-2014.aspx. The average increase from 2014-2015 is 5.3 person; see https://www.naceweb.org/s04172013/average-starting-salary.aspx.

[5] Top-Paid Business Majors at the Bachelor's and Master's Levels, February 18, 2015, National Association of Colleges and Employers. URL: https://www.naceweb.org/s02182015/top-paid-business-majors-2015.aspx

[6] 10 High-Paying Flexible Jobs, January 15, 2013, Forbes. URL: http://www.forbes.com/sites/jacquelynsmith/2013/01/15/10-high-paying-flexible-jobs/

[7] PMI Fact File, March 2015, PMI Today, Project Management Institute Inc.

[viii] Miller, S., Hickson, D., and Wilson, D., (2008). From strategy to action: Involvement and influence in top level decisions. Long Range Planning, 41(6), 606-628.

[ix] Speculand, R., (2009). Six necessary mind shifts for implementing strategy. Business Strategy Series, 10, (3), 167-172.

[x] Economist Intelligence Unit Special Report, (2013). Why good strategies fail: Lessons for C-suite. The Economist.

[xi] Corboy, M., and O'Corrbui, D., (1999). The seven deadly sins of strategy. Management Accounting, 77(10), 29-30.

[xii] Beer, M., and Nohria, N., (2000). Cracking the code of change. Harvard Business Review, 78, 133-194.

[xiii] Raps, A., (2004). Implementing strategy. Strategic Finance, 85(12), 48-53.

[xiv] Sull, D., Homkes, R., & Sull, C., (2015). "Why strategy execution unravels - and what to do about it." Harvard Business Review, 93(3), 57-66.

[xv] Bureau of Labor Statistics, U.S. Department of Labor, Occupational Handbook Outlook for Management Analysts, 2014-15 Edition, http://www.bls.gov/ooh/business-and-financial/management-analysts.htm

[xvi] International Project Management Association, Wikipedia. URL: http://en.wikipedia.org/wiki/International_Project_Management_Association

REMEMBER THE SPECIAL BONUS

Register this book at www.pmoadvisory.com/product-registration and receive a FREE version of our very popular "Quick Sheet for Project Managers".

Made in the USA
Monee, IL
23 November 2020